MW01244376

THE WILDERNESS OF CHANGE

A Guidebook To Light Your Way Along The Path Of Change

Copyright © 2015 by Lorin R. Walker

9 SW 260th Road
Warrensburg Missouri 64093

Published by Walker Armada

ISBN-13: 978-1511816687
ISBN-10: 1511816686

BISAC: Self-Help / Personal Growth / General

All rights reserved. No part of this book may be reproduced or transmitted in any form or by any means, electronic or mechanical, including photocopying, recording, or by any information storage and retrieval system, without the written permission of Lorin R. Walker, except where permitted by law.

FIRST EDITION

by LORIN R. WALKER

Becky —
I am so happy that you
decided to hook up with
this family. I take joy in
Knowing you + so appreciate
the good care you are taking
of our son. May these pages
bring wisdom. Love
Dad
2016

DEDICATION

Eternal gratitude to the good, great women in my life: Lin, Jo Anne
and my mother Verna

ACKNOWLEDGEMENTS

I estimate that over 500 people helped me generate this book, starting with my earliest teachers, and including mentors, coaches, friends, parents, grandparents, clients and students. Thanks to all of them. I have forgotten some names, and I am sure some lessons, but cherish what stuck.

Special thanks to the ten brave volunteers, ages 21-71, four men and six women, who signed on at my invitation via Facebook and other means, and persevered throughout the 14 months I spent composing and recomposing this book, while they tried it on and stretched it into better shape.

Here's the original Facebook invitation:

"Seeking 10 people to test drive a new personal change methodology, part of a book I am writing. I promise new stuff for you to try approx every three weeks, in return for a little report on how it went. Let me know if you want in."

The invitation still stands, tho I seek 1,000.

Thanks to Micah Walker, who enlivened my interest in the writing exercises in the book *Writing Better Lyrics*, by Pat Pattison, which helped me bring prose that was laced more with visceral/visual feel and imagery... and which taught me writing exercises to wake up the muse on early, cold, dark mornings.

To Phil Lunceford, who repeatedly replaced the anxiety of creation with the spirit and sanity of same.

To Charlotte Shelton, President and CEO of Unity, who convinced me I had something worth sharing.

To my siblings, sons and daughter, for their love and support, and for giving me a live laboratory and plenty of candid feedback in all my lived-in, just-barely-in-time learning. To my brother, Clair Walker, who stood at my side in the flesh and otherwise, in the coldest, darkest wee hours, as my eyes ached for glimmers of dawn, and instructed me to eat protein at crucial, shaky moments. To Charlotte Drake, confidante, sister and friend.

Rogers George III, for his kind and skillful correction of my sometimes goofy grammar.

Ed Murphy, who crafted the manuscript into shape for publication.

Henry and Sue Kester, who fed me good home cooking in an extended family atmosphere, and encouraged me to write the prologue, to give spirit, life and context to the book.

All those who encouraged and allowed my 50-plus wilderness adventures the last dozen decades, where I was privileged to capture the photographs on the cover and the inner pages.

Aaron McCann and the five McCann women, who kept me biking, hiking and eating well during the darkest days.

To Denise, who fed my soul.

To my son Spencer, who exerted his professional artistry and class to bring clarity and sparkle to these pages.

WHAT OTHERS SAY

"This book helped me fight through my natural impatience. I would make changes too fast and my anxiety would soar. Or change did not happen fast enough so I would be impatient and frustrated. By using the tools in this book, I have been more able to manage change at a rate I can absorb. Not so fast I am overwhelmed and not so slow that I lose focus."

CW, Idaho

"By signing up to participate in this personal change process... I am becoming more aware of change in my life and learning to becoming comfortable with it as something that is constant and always has the potential of creating opportunity for personal growth. The process I have signed up for is causing me to shift the value I have for change in my personal and professional life. So the big change in my life is my relationship with [former spouse]...My first response to this big change was, 'What can I do to make it better?' I tried a lot of different strategies only to find that nothing helped. So this was a change that ultimately was not in my control. In conclusion, this program has been helping in realizing that I'm not at fault for things that I could not control. Changing my focus from the change that changed my life, to how will I live my life despite unfair changes."

TA, Arizona

"Change has come easier for me than most people. Perhaps because my family moved regularly when I was young - and my mom and dad divorced 3 times before I reached my 16th birthday. I learned early in life to "go with the flow." But Lorin's directions on how to embrace change made me reflect and put meaning to each change I went through. I never planned to go through a painful divorce after 28 years - never planned to bury a husband after 15 years. I am an old lady now and have experienced many of life's trials. The skills I learned from his directions have been invaluable in coping with the changes that old age brings. Thank you, and God bless you all."

SB, Texas

"This is really helping me. I have always been a person who looks at change as a bad thing—I think I got that from my mom—she's a lot like that. This has helped me see that 'change is a good thing.' I am still using the advice from this book even several years later. Each time a big change comes, I look at is as something to be used for good rather than a thorn in my side. I find myself going back to several of the exercises from the book and using them, even forgetting that they came from the book. They have become part of my life...part of my coping strategies."

TR, Missouri

"I thoroughly enjoyed participating in these exercises. Some of them are designed to prepare us for change by improving our emotional and spiritual personal change resilience. Others actually help us successfully navigate change when it arrives, by getting us to both view the change objectively, and focus our thoughts and energies on important human relationships. The principles taught are eternal truths applicable to all."

EP, Texas

"I am a person that likes change. I often rearrange my furniture to give me a different perspective. Of course there is also change that has occurred in my life that I didn't like, such as when my daughter got married and she was no longer coming through the front door every day. It was a wonderful thing and exactly what I wanted for her, but I missed her. Then there is the kind of change associated with loss, which doesn't feel like a wonderful thing at all. Lorin's book helped me to understand myself a little better so that I can see the value in embracing whatever kind of change comes along. As he says, 'change is inevitable'. So learning to embrace and see the value in change helps us deal with something that is going to happen whether we want it to or not. It is a great read and re-read for anyone."

JM, Missouri

"I now try to be still when change happens. The book helped me see how the initial 'blast zone' of change passed and by not overreaction to the initial change 'flash,' I was able to help others through change and help myself through unanticipated change happenings."

SS, Kansas

"This change program has really helped me...So this has gone pretty good for me. I feel like I can keep up with the changes that I've undertaken and I have decreased my anxiety about change by realizing that it is normal and constant. The perpetual encouragement was great, I reviewed it every few days to re-motivate myself to continue."

JR, Missouri

CONTENTS

PROLOGUE

The phone call was ahead of schedule, and unwelcome.

"Lorin, I have cancer. It is going to kill me."

That was toward the middle of the phone call. It did not start that way. It started with my wife, Lin, saying, "The test was positive. I have a tumor on my pancreas. There are also some spots on my liver. We have an appointment with the oncologist Tuesday next week." She said other things that are lost in the mists of time and in the confusion of the unthinkable.

Whatever I said in response led my wife to declare her cancer in terms that were stark and unmistakable. As she always did, she cut through my fog of denial with a scalpel of well-placed syllables. I did not want to hear this news; even less did I want to hear it while seated on a bed far away from her side, in a gray, anonymous hotel room in Houston, Texas. I felt a weight of grief settle into my chest, as if a pair of giant hands were squeezing the air out of me. I shed silent tears while she was on the phone, and then when I hung up, my chest convulsed into heavy sobs. I sank to my knees. I prayed.

I am not proud of my first thoughts. My first reaction was to feel sorry for myself, for what I was losing. My next reaction was anger, for the tender companionship I was being forced to give up. Only then did I feel badly for Lin. Only then did I begin to think about the dark shadow pressing on her life and soul, of the anguish of her uncertain future of treatment, her pain, and giving up the things she loved most.

Looking back, the sequence and confluence of timing of this event were eerie in their perfect precision. For some time, I had been writing a self-help book, on personal change resilience, teaching how to embrace the energy of change and turn it to the benefit of self and loved ones. I had finished the manuscript a short time before, after months of work, and after many years of learning from experience and mentors. Little did I know that in preparing to write something that would help others cope with change, I was really writing something that would help me—I had been prepared through the writing process.

The onslaught of emotion and thought that washed over me in that lonely hotel room contained none of these insights.

This was all background, understood only in retrospect. The thought that came next, instead, imposed itself as an image—a flash-back to my father's cancer 12 years earlier, to the three and one half months I had spent at his bedside, caring for him during his last days on the planet, daily assaulted with the emotion of loss as one of my best friends on earth slipped the bonds of his earthly sojourn. The flashback was not comforting.

As I arose from my knees, my phone beeped at me. The screen informed me of a text from Roy Grant, a physician friend from Storm Lake, Iowa, one of my most faithful backpacking companions. He wanted to talk backpacking. I had a few minutes before my business dinner, and placed a call to him. He had a question regarding where to backpack in Colorado. I had questions of a different sort. Rather than my telling him about Colorado wilderness paths, he ended up educating me about my path—through the upcoming wilderness of terminal cancer. He immediately understood my feelings and situation. "Wow, you just found out. You must be reeling. You are just absorbing the news. You may not want to talk much now. But we can talk now if you want, and we can talk later. I am always available at any time. I keep doctor's hours. We can talk later about my trip to the mountains; you have more important things on your mind." We spoke briefly. He was the first of my many angels of immaculate timing.

Then I experienced one of the most surreal occasions of my life. The Merriam-Webster dictionary defines surreal as "marked by the intense irrational reality of a dream". Dreamlike, I hung up the phone and took the elevator downstairs to a dinner with my boss and other business colleagues. My shaken mind was still struggling to absorb this unwelcome and life-altering information. I was not prepared to share any intimation of how my life had just changed forever. I acted as if it were just a normal business dinner at the end of another normal working day. The evening continued to pass like a dream of unreality. At one point my boss asked the three of us to state what we thought would be something that our company could undertake that would be the most meaningful and high-contribution way to spend our corporate time. I have no remembrance whatsoever of what I said, nor what others said. That was the first of many surreal moments.

In time, surreal became real, and I learned to cope with the unthinkable, as I applied the principles in the book you are holding in your hands to my own changed-forever life. The book became a warm Santa Ana wind blowing at my back, as Lin and I ran the can't-turn-back marathon to the finish line of her life.

My original aim in writing this book was to elucidate principles to help people feel better about themselves and be more competent and at peace in the face of life's changes. I wanted to outline a practical methodology to transform the energy of change into positive energy for the benefit of self and of loved ones. As I wrote, I drew from my experience of 27 years as a therapist, consultant, and coach to individuals and couples, and to leaders of the Fortune 100; as a community volunteer leader, and as the co-parent of seven energetic and independent children, and grandfather to a half-dozen more.

I identified four types of change—expected, both positive and negative; and unexpected, both positive and negative. I endeavored to teach how to transform and redirect the energy of any type of change for increased personal power in bringing about further positive change for self and loved ones.

I was suddenly in the midst of a type 4 change—unexpected, unwelcome. So in a way, I was my own angel of immaculate timing. The principles took on powerful life on the center stage of my mind, just in time. Even though these were principles I had acquired through my own life experience, and I had written about them before in bits and snatches, I had never before captured them so succinctly.

In attempting to become a healer to others, I had to become my own physician. The book became my inoculation against a most challenging change. I stopped writing the book, and started living the book. Adhering to its principles took me sledding across the surface of the avalanche of cancer, safely on top, not ground under by its deadly, tumbling expanse.

A short four days before the phone call, we had been sitting side by side in her dream car, which I had just purchased for her, a Volkswagen "heavenly blue" bug. I sat in the driver's seat, as she did not trust herself to drive at the moment. She held my hand and gazed at me with those oh-so-heavenly-blue and clear eyes, and spoke unforgettable words. She had just come from the MRI, transported through the machine's bowels as it looked at all manner of parts of her body. She was silent when she came out and took me in tow from where I sat in the waiting room. We stepped out of the building into the rays of the midmorning sun, the warmth on my face belying the cold I felt in my belly.

She sat in the passenger seat and said, "All signs are that it is cancer. The doctor will look at it and confirm in two days. I am so sorry." She was apologizing for the pain she knew it would cause me. She was apologizing for her early exit from our marriage and our life.

She was who she was, always thinking of others before thinking of herself. I told her she did not have to apologize; that we would handle whatever came. Looking back, we stepped together into an unknown, dark continent at that moment. Our mutual grieving commenced—but it was nothing compared to what was to come.

There are many solemn jokes in the universe. Youth being wasted on the young is one. Marriage is another (putting marriages in the hands of newlyweds!). Take two immature people of perhaps completely different familial and often regional cultures. Throw them together into an intimate, forever-committed relationship. Bind them together by law. Throw sex and children and education and vocation and pregnancy and in-laws and mortgages and car payments and sickness into the mix. Oh, and press these two hapless souls together, like two different genera of leaves set one on top of the other—clamp them between the pages of the heavy book of one of the most self-centered "me" cultures in the history of the planet, and watch what happens as their lives press tightly together. Open the book from time to time to let in a little light and fresh air, but mostly keep them in the dark. That any marriage whatsoever survives is a great wonder.

In our own personal marvelous joke, we made mistakes. Along with the joys of marriage, we felt the jolts of marriage. As Lin said in a letter to me that she dictated shortly before her death:

"We've spent almost 40 years together and they have been the joy of my life, and even though we've had our ups and downs and misunderstandings, and oh, just life in general, for the most part our life together has been very happy and I'm so glad I met you and married you. I love you very much... I didn't want to leave you this early... I just want you to know that I do love you and I can always come back to that primary relationship. I'm grateful for having this time together. It hasn't always been easy, it hasn't always been sweet, and anybody who's married knows that, but it has been a good experience, and I'm grateful for that."

I was grateful for her acceptance and maturity, but was still determined to erase in a few months all my mistakes of our 39 years together. I was actually able to do that. Or rather, Lin did it for both of us:

One morning, fairly early, Lin and I were talking in bed. I was in a self-critical mood, trying in 10 minutes to erase the effects of what I saw as 4 decades of imperfection in my part of our marriage, trying to eradicate all the memories of my sometimes impatience, sometimes immaturity, and often self-centeredness. In other words, the stuff of most marriages.

She fastened her eyes straight upon mine, and then, as recorded in my journal, said: "Lorin, I have had a good life. I have had a happy life. There are no loose ends. I feel complete."

I stopped looking back almost entirely in that moment of clarity. Her words became my rallying declaration and goal—to live my life so that at the end I would be able to make a similar declaration. And when is the end of my life? It could be in 10 years, or it could be in 10 minutes, meaning that I must be able at all moments to make this declaration. That is my goal and my hope. The principles in this book help me to fulfill that declaration. It will help you also as you learn and apply its principles.

You might not face a change so dramatic and negative as cancer. Your change might have to do with graduating from college or a certification program and now needing to apply the new knowledge to new circumstances. Or you might be facing the birth of a child, or a new job, or the myriad other changes that life lovingly sends our way. No matter what the change, this book will help you rally your strength and motivation for your good and the good of those around you.

One experience especially stands out that illustrates the point. One early morning, I could not sleep, and left her side, her breath uneven, coming in short, jerky snatches. I closed the bedroom door softly behind me. I sat in the living room, my bare feet on the hardwood floor, and pondered our situation, trying to come to grips with the surreal but deadly phantoms of our life. I do not remember my exact thoughts of that moment, but I do remember what happened next.

I heard the creak of the bedroom door opening. She came into the living room, wearing her favorite pink nightgown. I stood. Her eyes studded with tears, she uttered the words, "I just hate this!" As I stood, she melted into my arms. "I hate it too," I said. We stood that way, in tearful silence, for a long time. Then, we "went down to the creek, washed away our tears, and moved on." We moved forward, directly into the change, like the ship that, in the last extremity, instead of running before the gale, turns and faces it squarely, straight into the surge of the waves.

This was one of many such coping-with-change moments. She would often comment on how strange it was to her that there was something, quite small at the moment, growing inside her body, that would soon take her life, and that there was nothing that we could do about it. And it kept growing,

This was what I have identified as a Type IV change—in both our lives. This was a change both unwelcome and unexpected. This was a change that was rocking our universe. This is one of the prime topics of the book.

In our own personal circumstance, we clove to each other, clasped hands tightly, faced forward, and walked resolutely toward the muted green glow of her life's exit sign, determined to put a well-crafted capstone upon the apex of the final doorway of our earth-life together. The soft, surreal, unblinking glow of that sign tinted the air around every corner, hinting at the shortness of our time together.

Short months later, surreal became real, as I stepped up to her silver-gray casket placed just below the brow of the hill at the country cemetery, next to the lake, under a blue spring sky smudged with clouds. Carefully, one by one, I extracted yellow roses (symbolic of Texas, her adopted state) from the lovely bouquet on top of the casket and distributed them to the people she held most dear. After handing out a dozen or so roses, I looked around and saw a hundred people still gathered in solemn support, sad to see her go but buoyed up by our mutual love and caring and the lingering energy of the positive, tearful, joyful funeral service of an hour earlier.

As I walked around near the casket, my newly-polished black shoes making temporary imprints on the green grass near her body's final resting place, I was surprised at the positive energy I felt, but grateful to be able to express it. I felt buoyed up and inclined to ease the pain of others. As we lingered at the site, each taking leave in his or her own way, I felt a magnet of love and appreciation drawing me to each person and cluster of people in turn.

I shared with them the good cheer that I felt, the calm assurance and solid hope that brought light to all the recesses of my heart. My brother Mike, who by profession is an editor, had been taking it all in with his chronicler's eye—he wrote soon thereafter in a Blog post how I had been "there and everywhere, comforting each visitor who was in need of comfort". My sentiments of reaching out were genuine; it was not an act. I felt badly for them. I was living my book.

I did not realize it at the time, but I had made some decisions. I had decided in many small ways to embrace this mighty change. I had decided that the rest of my life would be not a dirge, but a grand parade. Others might try to rain on my parade, but I was still going to sponsor a great parade. I had decided, through my eternal companion's death, to be more alive. I decided that the next chapter of my life was going to be the most satisfying adventure I had ever had.

Many are helping to man my parade and get the horses prancing and the clowns dancing and the fire engines fired up. For example, my second son, Micah, said some great things in a conversation that we had shortly after her death, when the loss and the grieving were hitting us both like a leaden hammer-blow. He said, "I think mom would want us to be happy. She would want us to be engaged with life, and moving forward."

I recommend Micah's words to all. May they define your path as you move forward into the changes that you face in your own personal rendition of life on this planet.

INTRODUCTION:

Changing For Good

Change brings growth, power and happiness.

This program is about change. Your change. And change in the world around you. In this program, your change is the foreground, and change in the world around you is the background. This background becomes your source of stimulation and energy and contributive resistance (like lifting weights to grow stronger).

This program is also about growth and happiness. Your growth and happiness. And, by extension, that of those around you. There is a tight linkage among change, growth, and happiness.

We will manage change, or it will manage (read manhandle) us. Change, well directed, is the wellspring of growth and happiness. Change, undirected or left to chance, might also bring growth and happiness. But there is no guarantee.

This program espouses temporary pain for permanent gain. Choose the pain intelligently, and the gain is chosen in that same moment.

Change is here to stay. Permanently. As I write this, I sit on a chair that sits on a concrete pad that sits on an earth that is rotating at a tremendous rate of speed. At the same time, the earth is revolving around the sun at enormous velocity. The sun is speeding around the maw of the Milky Way. The Milky Way...you get the idea. Oh, and all the while the concrete pad that the chair is on is deteriorating, cracking, shifting, slowly turning to dust. And the hill on which the pad sits is moving, at glacial pace, particle by particle, into the valley below my house. And the trees outside are casting down seeds and nutrients (dead leaves), and daffodil bulbs are multiplying and taking hold four inches under the earth and readying themselves for a glorious Spring. And the squirrels are multiplying. And the wood of the chair........again, you get the idea. Change is more constant than time.

Even the days are constantly changing. No two consecutive days are the same length. Daylight is always shorter, or longer. Change is the new stability.

No wonder we all feel dizzy from time to time, or wish that things would slow down a bit.

There is an alternative to dizziness: conscious channeling of change energy to the benefit of self and of those you love.

This program invites you to go directly at change, so to speak—to embrace (or grapple with) the energy of change—to engage in a personal change methodology until parts of it become parts of you. To think, feel, and do in new ways, until the entire personal process of change, the movement of growth, becomes habitual.

Making the most of change is an important life skill. Through applying this program, you can learn that skill.

Many people experience change as stress and fear of loss. They experience it as awkward and uncomfortable. A threat. An interruption.

A few experience change as novel and exciting. As opportunity. When things don't turn out the way they anticipated, they say, "How fascinating!". They learn from it. They see change as an invitation to growth, greater understanding and joy.

My opinion is that if you resist change too strongly, if you try to hang on to all that you already have too tightly, you run the risk of losing most of what you care about.

The goal is increased Personal Change Resilience.

Personal change resilience is the power to transmute the energy of change to the benefit of yourself and those you love.

Change-resilient people:

1. Replace the energy of worry with the energy of focused action.
2. Look to change as a source of strength and creativity.
3. Display serenity and resolve in the face of change.
4. Do not sweat the small stuff.
5. Habitually find ways to serve in the midst of disruption and dislocation.
6. Gladly invest energy in supporting others through change.
7. See the big picture and are calm and reconciled to larger, longer-term outcomes.
8. Do not excuse themselves because of others' weakness.
9. Do not blame others for their own personal weakness.
10. Look for opportunity in change.

11.   As a reflex, use the energy of change to bring benefit to self and to those they love.

12.   Do all they can in the face of change, then await the results in peace.

These are results worth working hard to attain!

This program is structured to build habits of strength.

I have identified sixteen vital change resilience skills, or principles, through more than 25 years of research and experience with individuals, families, and organizations. Each of these is both additive and multiplicative; in other words, they build on each other, and the whole becomes more than the sum of the parts. Each principle is a call to action. Each asserts you have the power in you to choose for yourself, to consciously sculpt or rebuild yourself and the world around you.

This program is not a quick fix, though quick fixes occur from time to time as you apply the methodology. It is designed as a process that takes place over time. The process includes a preparatory stage, which is described in this chapter. Then work on the 16 principles begins. Each personal change resilience skill can be significantly improved in 2-3 weeks. The capstone is a sustainability phase which will serve to consolidate your improvements.

The 16 Principles of Personal Change Resilience are:

1.   Embrace change

2.   Magnify empowering life assumptions

3.   Embrace the law of the harvest

4.   Cultivate positive stress

5.   Reframe bad/good

6.   Pursue personal talent

7.   Feed your self-esteem

8.   Drive closure

9.   Learn constantly

10.   Design fulfillment structures

11.   Cultivate humor

12.   Exercise stewardship

13.   Invent projects

14.   Nurture positive relationships

15.   Create threads of stability

16.   Exert intentionality

Change is a multiplier of growth and happiness:

We live in a world of classifications: good, better, best, worst. Upgrade 3.1. Release 5.6.3. We classify some change as positive, some as negative.

This program is about classifying all change as positive. All change can be welcome. You will experience many, many changes in your life. You might as well turn the change energy into a force propelling you in the direction that you need or want to go.

The program also assumes that the rate of change in the world, including in your world, is accelerating (more opportunity). One hundred years ago, or even 50 years ago, one career, one organization, per lifetime, was the norm. Now the norm is four to five careers per lifetime, spread across even more organizations, and the rate is increasing all the time. This gives more opportunity for the multiplication of growth and happiness.

The parts of each chapter build on each other for immediate improvement.

PRINCIPLES

First, in each chapter you will see a short statement of principle. Principles are sets of rules, doctrines, insights—in short, laws of life—that advocate certain motives and actions. The principle will be accompanied by a picture of wilderness. The wilderness is a metaphor for our journey through the wilderness-opportunity of change.

SONGLINE

The next section is a songline. A songline is a rich set of instructions containing the power and wisdom of experience. Each songline is designed to keep the explorer (you) on track across the unknown wilderness of change.

Songlines can be songs, poems, words, paintings, natural or man-made objects, and symbols. Songlines, in the original use, were created, sung, and memorized by Australian aboriginal people to assist in finding their way across the Outback. From an early age, songlines play a vital role in educating children. They convey wisdom: they explain how the land came to be shaped and inhabited; how one is to behave and why; where to find certain foods and remedies; how to find one's way across the wilderness.

The songlines for the personal change resilience methodology will be expressed as sets of illustrations, explanations, life experiences and anecdotes. The songline is meant to be both instructive and memorable—so that the basics can be absorbed and exist and persist in your mind and spirit, giving meaning that is always available, no matter where you are.

The Wisdom of K. Hieronymus

In each module you will find a capsule of wisdom from K. Hieronymus. The Kestrel Hieronymus is a creature of myth, with special insight into the human condition. His advice will be succinct and sage.

After the songline is an explanation of how to apply this principle, how it might play out in your life, how the principle actually takes hold to transform change energy into personal growth energy. This section sets the stage for your opportunity to focus attention on personal action and growth.

LIFE TOOLS™

Then comes the invitation to action—Life Tools. Your choice, at least one. These are things you can start right away, and perhaps finish in a day, though many will take longer. Most you can complete in a few weeks.

With use, a Life Tool may evolve into a principle—a personal rule of thumb that you can apply to many situations. For the principles you most desire to master, I suggest you do more than one. Or if you are an unrepentant over-achiever, by all means do them all. But only one is necessary to fulfill the principle. Practicing the principle by applying a Life Tool makes it a part of you, a tool that can be used for life.

APPENDIX

Next comes the appendix, which will be consistently the same—a bit of a call to action, some new information, repetitive encouragement, reminders.

SUMMARY

Last of all is a short summary of the principle, for ready reference.

Pushing through resistance brings success.

This "change system" is designed for immediate action, persistent application, and life enrichment.

But here's what will happen: your life will happen, with all the unexpected changes and challenges that always happen in your life. This program takes place inside of that. Sometimes in spite of that. Emotions will both sidetrack and propel you. Both committed and incidental relationships will clamor for your attention. You will find yourself by turns excited, resisting, giving up, recommitting, feeling guilty, feeling elated, bored, satisfied, energetic. The trick is to persist despite all challenge and emotion.

Life won't just stand still while you fulfill this change program. That river will just keep on running. And: if you really do start to make some changes, someone around you might get nervous, and might even try to stop you.

Another thing can happen: I believe that when you truly make a commitment, the universe shifts to help you fulfill your commitment. "Teachers" appear. You get unexpected phone calls that further your purposes. You run into people you have not seen for a long time, and what they are doing might trouble you (jealousy?) or inspire you, or what they say might offend you—or propel you into effective action. Resources and books will fall your way. And sometimes things around you will fall apart. Relationships might crash, and even burn. People might get angry for apparently no reason. Machines might break down. You might experience a piling-on effect. I see all of these things as the universe creating a clearing for you, or creating a bubble for you, within which you can build something new.

As you work to change in the face of change, all of your old habits of resisting authority, fearing loss, fearing change (based on your visceral memories of all the times change didn't turn out so well), will come into play.

You might even find yourself resenting me for introducing this program into your life. But if you desire, that heroic part of you that exercises faith and takes on new things will step forward and carry the day.

Some principles will speak to you more than others. Some, you will go through, check the box, do the assignment just because you promised yourself you would. Boring but OK—you kept your commitment.

Others will light up your imagination and your life. You will take action, and be surprised by joy. You might even be a little scared and nervous at the beginning, but you will keep on. These are the ones that will stick with you for a long, long time. You will end up teaching them by precept or by example to your children and friends. They will become part of who you are.

Apply three simple keys for success in increasing change resilience:

Key #1—Schedule time for starting new things:

You greatly enhance your success by simply setting aside time to do the program. Literally write it down on your schedule. Decide a time when you will read the installment each time, designate by when you will choose your task, and when you will start. Decide when you will send in your report. Progress comes when you schedule time for it.

To be able to do the program, you will likely have to take something else off your schedule to make time and free up energy. For example, to make time to write this program, I let my four photography magazine subscriptions lapse, and have delayed certain associated activities.

Key #2—Set up a Reminder System:

Change your visible/physical environment to remind yourself that you are trying something new. Design this system yourself, and apply it to each principle. It will remind you, amidst the busyness of your life, that you have embarked upon a personal change adventure.

Your mnemonic can be as simple as an index card taped to your bathroom mirror, a special coin or object placed in your pocket, a saying taped to the refrigerator door (where else!?), a band around your wrist, a picture of a "new you," a dot of fingernail polish on your watch face.

Make it something you will notice frequently throughout the day. Each time you notice it, remind yourself of your commitment. As you progress through each principle, you might need to change up your system a bit to retain its freshness and power. You are learning how to proactively change, especially how to proactively embrace change and change's attendant power.

Key #3—Do the Work:

Just keep moving. And if one thing does not work, or life asserts its own agenda and you do not keep your commitment to yourself, do not permanently give up. Try something else, set a new goal, keep working. Put in the time. Remember, you are learning to be a pro—a professional change-maker. Pros show up and take on the task, consistently, day after day, without fail. That is what pros do. Be a pro.

That said, there are times when you should stop (temporarily), and ponder redirection. This program takes time. Your time. It is not a quick and magic pill. The reading of each installment should take from 10 to 20 minutes. The Life Tool(s) will take whatever time you give them. You might need to delay temporarily, or commit differently.

But do not stop. You have a reason why you have chosen to participate in a personal change program. Do not lightly take that opportunity away from yourself.

Get started by doing the following two exercises:

To get into the mindset of proactive personal change resilience, complete the sentences below:

- When I think about change, I ...
- Change is ...
- A recent change that was easy for me was ...
- A change that has been hard for me is ...
- An example of a positive change that I have experienced is ...
- An example of a negative change that I have experienced is ...
- I resist change when ...
- Things that help me change are ...
- Three things in my life I would really like to see change are ...
- If everything goes well, the changes I will see in five years are ...

If anything in particular occurs to you as a result of answering these questions, jot it down, and think about what it is telling you.

Put change in its place by applying the "Change Posture Grid":

Types of Change	Welcome	Unwelcome
Anticipated	**Type I**	**Type II**
Unanticipated	**Type III**	**Type IV**

Examples are:

Anticipated and Welcome (Type I):

As an example, four years ago, when you embarked on your bachelor's degree, you knew the time would come when you would receive your degree. Now it has come. What a change! You do not go to class tomorrow. But what will you do?

For this type of change, look forward, anticipate, relish, and remember.

Anticipated, but Unwelcome (Type II):

As an example, you knew the time would come when your car would wear down to the point of not being worth repairing. This has been one of your favorite cars, but now you must give it up. But for what?

For this type of change, prepare, endure, and learn.

Unanticipated, but Welcome (Type III):

As an example, you completed a tough project over the last two weeks. Out of the blue, the owner of the company gives you a cash bonus. This has never happened before. But how will you spend it? To pay down debt, or to take your spouse out to dinner?

For this type of change, quickly decide how to take advantage, act, relish, and remember.

Unanticipated and Unwelcome (Type IV):

As an example, through a series of circumstances, you arrive exactly two minutes late to check in for your flight. The next flight available for your class of ticket is in two days. And that is how it is. You will have to skip seeing an old friend, and must make many other changes to your plans. You hope this becomes a character-building experience.

For this type of change, take personal responsibility for making the most of it, stop complaining and whining as quickly as possible, ask for help, don't play "if only." Let go of the past and focus on specific possible future outcomes.

Realize that any change creates stress and the necessity to make decisions. Types I and III are easiest, perhaps, but still have their challenges. Maturity says, "Find the opportunity in all change".

Pick 3 recent changes and classify them. Once you have done this, you are prepared to begin to pursue and reap the benefits of the 16 Personal Change Resilience principles!

Briefly describe the change	Type of change	What you did	What you could have done differently

PRINCIPLE 1:

Embrace Change

Change is the ground we walk on and the air we breathe. In our time, the forces and frequency of change are accelerating. This is a great personal opportunity. Managing change is a misnomer—change exists and persists. We live in it; we do not manage it. We do not manage the medium of our existence. However, we can manage ourselves through change. Accept change as normal, natural, eternal and desirable—peace, happiness and growth will be the result.

SONGLINE
Learn to navigate the wilderness of change

It was not a good day when I was let go from my job in a corporate downsizing, and then arrived home (early!) to find that a handwritten letter from my father had just arrived in the mail. His simple message was— "I have just been diagnosed with terminal cancer. I have very few months to live." The cry of rage and grief that bulled its way out through my tight-clenched lips barely expressed what I felt deep in my gut. I was in my home office, collapsed to my knees and bent over my hard wooden chair attempting prayer, door tightly closed against the demons of the dark, when the noise erupted from my throat, and my good wife had to explain to the kids, rooms away, that I had just received news that my father was soon to die. Many things changed that day. It was the beginning of sorrows. And the beginning of a long, dullish journey to a new day. A journey I managed both poorly and well.

Totally thrown off balance by the change wrought by the multi-assault, only later did I comprehend the blessing of having a large space of free time, severance-supported, to spend the last days of his mortal life in the presence of and caring for my best male friend on this planet.

Over the course of four months, which ended in my father's death, my understanding deepened. At the end, I wrote in my journal, treating the experience as if it were an allegory:

What if you started praying for a positive life change—diligently—and you had a vivid, intense dream. You are in the mountains. You climb all day amongst rock and ice and alpine meadows. At the summit of the tallest mountain you meet a sage, a teacher of life. He promises:

- Positive change in your life.
- A space of time to renew/cement your relationship with siblings.
- The chance to record the stories of your father's (colorful) life.
- That you would learn to give service at a whole new level.
- The opportunity to join with your mother in a project of great significance.
- The opportunity to spend extended time in the Idaho Rocky Mountains that you love so dearly.

But to do that, you would be required to make many sacrifices. As you try to decide whether or not to accept this proposition, you ponder:

- Sacrifice means giving up something good for something better.
- Before you can have a blessing, you need to clear a space for it.
- The best and most fundamental and most lasting sacrifice is that of a broken heart—not angry nor resentful at setbacks—and a contrite, willing spirit.

Are you ready to go ahead in pursuit of this change?

In your dream, you decide quickly. You decide to go ahead. You wake up. In short order, in real life, the changes and sacrifices begin:

- You lose your job in a corporate downsizing.
- Your computer hard drive crashes.
- Your pet cat is run over in the street and killed.
- Your wife undergoes major surgery, while you struggle to take care of five teenage boys, solo, for some time, in the midst of a job search.
- Your mailbox is taken out by an errant car.
- You move to Idaho and install yourself into the bedroom next to your father's room.
- You are deprived of the companionship of your wife and children for extended periods of time.
- You totally give up uninterrupted sleep and pull many, many all-nighters for months on end.
- You arise at 5–5:30 every morning to fix breakfast for your father, day after day after day.
- You take your turn cleaning up vomit.
- You experience the pain of witnessing your father's pain.
- You wash your father's feet.
- You lose your best male friend.

Eventually, I learned to endure and embrace these hardships with courage, even joy. The bad times became good times, though not without cost. The promises listed above were eventually all fulfilled; my hopes were realized. But that first night I was much, much less than hopeful, and much, much less than courageous.

These change experiences taught me that we must find our true path in and through change. Even as change finds its true path in and through us.

Learning to generate good times out of "bad" times is the primary life skill. This skill will be called for again and again, increasingly the case in our world of accelerating change and tumult.

Fortunately, the skill to embrace change can be learned, but not in the abstract. It must be learned through the toil of daily experience. It must be learned proactively, as we move forward with courage and tackle the challenges that are before us. As we move forward, and the ground beneath us begins to buckle and quake with the shockwaves of change, we learn to step lightly and safely. We learn to proceed according to the 16 Principles of Personal Change Resilience.

When we stop resisting necessary change and start embracing it instead, positive transformation, peace, growth, and happiness begin.

APPLICATION
Employ this principle to benefit you and those you love

Change happens. Change happens and will continue to happen. What the changing environment doesn't do to you, you will do to yourself: most of us strive to live in a world of evolution and improvement. And how you handle change determines your degree of happiness and growth.

Change is a normal and natural part of life. Without it, there is no progress. There is no gain. There is also no yogurt, no alternation of daylight, twilight, and darkness. There is no springtime, no autumn. And also, of course, there is no deterioration, no loss. No new wrinkles, no new body aches and pains. No character building experiences.

Only two questions matter: in the face of this mad assault upon your serenity, will you be courageous, or will you be cowardly? Courage says, "Pick yourself up, dust yourself off, go down to the creek, wash the tears from your eyes, and get back to the business of life." Cowardice says, " Find someone to blame, exercise your right to complain, retreat from the opportunity, wallow in as much self-pity as others will endure; stretch the why-me envelope as much as possible."

Unprepared-for, unanticipated, unexpected change will throw you for a loop and rock your world. It may even grind you to dust.

Well-prepared-for, anticipated, girded-up-the-loins-against change will throw you for a loop and rock your world. It may even grind you to dust.

The trick is what you do with the dust. Add a little sweat and vinegar and tears, and you make a primal paste that can be sculpted into something unique and useful and maybe even beautiful. Yours is the choice.

Before our first child was born, we did our best to prepare for this change ahead of time. We prepared a place for the child to sleep, we had a crib, diapers, miniature clothing. We knew way ahead of time when the child would be born. We discussed many times how we would handle it. But when the event occurred, the change was immensely more jarring and difficult than anticipated. We had not predicted the amount of sleep loss. We had not prepared for the time required for maintenance. We had not anticipated the reaction of our pet dachshund. The stress was enormously greater than anticipated. But slowly, or at times quickly, we made the adjustment. We learned to work with sleep deprivation. We learned to physically and emotionally take care of this little soul. We learned, gradually, the joy of welcoming another human into the close circle of our lives. Decades later, we are still learning, adjusting, and enjoying.

This change was anticipated. Not all are. There are different kinds of change. Sometimes change comes at you in furious fashion, like a meteor shower. No matter how hard you try to dodge and duck, some of that change will hit you hard. You will rub the salve of comfort into your bruises, you will retreat to lick your wounds.

Sometimes change comes at you in slow-dance fashion. It steals over you softly and quietly, a barely visible fog that grows little by little; before you realize it, you are walking through thick, damp, gray soup. Or drowning.

I repeat,

You do not manage change; change manages, or rather, manhandles you.

When you go mano a mano with change, change always wins. It throws you for a loop, no matter how well practiced and prepared you think you are.

You cannot control whether or not change happens. You can resist, or you can ingest and embrace it. You can waste the dynamic energy of change, or you can harness it. The choice is yours.

The goal always is to ingest change, like you ingest food, letting it nourish and bring vitality and energy to every cell of our body. The goal always is to embrace the energy of change like you embrace growing up, as children. During the first 10 or 20 years of our lives, most of us yearn for change—to be bigger, older, to grow up and become a big boy, a big girl. And we do change and mature. Then, sadly, many of us want to slow down the progress of change.

Change begs for sacrifice, which is the main driver of progress. Sacrifice means giving up something good and sure for

The Wisdom of K. Hieronymus

Three examples of the constant change that surrounds us are the continual earth-shifting and magma-bubbling of the globe we stand on, our bodies constantly sloughing off old cells and manufacturing new cells, and the stars in feverish galactic flux.

Even as we stand where we now stand, we are hurtling around the sun at 67,062 mph—and spinning with the earth as it moves upon its axis, and going along for the (fast) ride with the rest of the galaxy, rushing toward the Andromeda galaxy at about 670,000 mph. We are immersed in change; we will become embalmed in it if we cling too tightly to "things as they are and must remain." Bottom line, don't resist; change will happen to us no matter how tightly we close our eyes and wish it away.

something better and uncertain. If you want something different to happen, you must make a space for it. Making the space, to use a gardener's analogy, is akin to pulling up the plants that are already there, and planting new seeds. The already-there plants may seem beautiful, but they must be sacrificed—compared to the new growth, they are weeds.

But change seldom happens according to exact plan and specification. You must always be open and expectant, planning, monitoring, acting and readjusting.

LIFE TOOLS™

Use consistently until they become your tools for life

1. Examine the change present in your life right now. Name the change, using the list of synonyms in the appendix and decide what flavor the various changes are. Naming the change will heighten power over the change, just as when Adam named the animals.

2. "Straighten your sock drawer" (take stock of your current material possessions, your "stuff"—throw away, give away, release to the universe).

3. Create a quiet space in your life to live with the reality or possibility of an actual change that is in your life, now or in the near future. For example, while contemplating a possible or real change in your life, welcome or unwelcome, wash the car. By hand. With a garden hose. And a bucket of sudsy water. Or engage in some other mundane activity. As you do this, contemplate how the ways in which this change might affect you. What would embracing it look like?

4. Accept the fact that change is normal, natural and desirable. Cultivate an attitude of being ready for the next change. Five days in a row, say something like the following to yourself (silently—don't spook the neighbors) as you step out the door in the morning: "I wonder what will change today for me and what the opportunity might be"?

5. The next time a change happens, be still and think, even if it is for no more than 20 seconds. Learn all you can from the (changed) present circumstances, and look forward to the next set of circumstances. Ask, "What can I learn from this change?" Make a list of possible "positive" and "negative" consequences. Inform others whom the change will affect. Quickly.

6. Consciously change your daily and/or weekly routine. Take a different route to work. Canoe on a lake at midnight. Try a food you have never eaten before. Start your day with reading something inspirational. Or end your day with the same. Do something out of order. Eat desert first, for example. Eat dinner for breakfast.

7. Take stock of the things that are OK in your life. Is there a place here for conscious sacrifice? Should you eliminate something to make a place for something better? As you take stock, make a list. Put a check next to the items that might bear "upgrading".

TRAPS

1. Avoid self-pity.

2. Avoid blaming others.

3. Avoid frenzy. Do not try to do everything at once to deal with the change.

4. Avoid creating change for the mere sake of change. Change is not always progress.

5. Be slow to accept advice re: what you should do about the change. The change belongs to you. It is yours. Own it and turn it to your advantage.

PERPETUAL ENCOURAGEMENT

Know that change is a process, a journey, if you will. You may not know where the next step will lead. The important thing is to just keep on walking. Take a swing. Take lots of swings. Don't be afraid to strike out. Eventually you do will hit something.

Do something. You can't correct a nothing."

APPENDIX

Different kinds of change call for different approaches. It helps to understand what type of change we are dealing with.

Verbs and nouns that denote different types of change are:

Transform, to make different in some particular, alter, to make radically different, to give a different position, course, or direction to, to replace with another, to make a shift from one to another, switch, to exchange for an equivalent sum, undergo a modification of, to put fresh clothes or covering on, to become different, to pass from one phase to another, to shift one's means of conveyance, transfer, to undergo transformation, transition, or substitution, vary, pass from the possession of one owner to that of another, modify, break away from sameness, alteration, difference, modification, redoing, refashioning, remaking, remodeling, revamping, revise, rework, amendment, correction, rectification; conversion, deformation, distortion, metamorphosis, mutation, transfiguration, transformation; fluctuation, oscillation, shift; displacement, replacement, substitution, adjustment, modulation, regulation, to put on different clothes.

SUMMARY

1. Change is the ground we walk on and the air we breathe.

2. We must learn to accept change as normal, natural, eternal, and desirable—peace, happiness, and growth are the result.

3. In our time, the forces and frequency of change are accelerating. This is a great personal opportunity.

4. All change creates stress. This can become the stress of growth, like the stress of growing up.

5. Change means sacrifice, which is the main driver of progress. Sacrifice means giving up something good and sure for something better and uncertain. If we want something different to happen, we must make a space for it.

6. Consciously accepting and embracing change is the main driver of peace and progress.

PRINCIPLE 2:

Magnify Empowering Life Assumptions

Be aware of and magnify your empowering life assumptions. These are the beliefs that strengthen you, that provide perspective in times of change and challenge. These are your nourishing beliefs about how life works, how you are "being treated" by life, what you expect of life—and what life expects of you.

SONGLINE
Learn to navigate the wilderness of change

A man once moved to a new town. He went there first on a scouting trip, to check out the town. He asked the first person he met, the owner of the local hardware store, what the people were like in the town.

The owner asked, "What are the people like in the town you are moving from?" The man answered, "They are not to be trusted. Bad neighbors. Very negative. I can't wait to leave." The owner said, "The people in this town are exactly like that!".

Another man, who was also moving to the town, arrived later that same day. The first person he met was the same hardware store owner. He asked him the same question; the same question came back—" What are the people like in the town you are moving from"? The man answered, "They are wonderful. Trustworthy. Good neighbors. Very positive. I hate to leave, but my work brings me here." The owner said, "The people in this town are exactly like that!".

The store owner's words were true in both instances. Each of these men was making a change. Believe the lesson of the story. Each will experience the new town quite differently. They experience change based on their life assumptions. The first held a negative life assumption; the second held an empowering life assumption.

In this installment we focus on your empowering life assumptions.

What you think of the people in the town where you live is only the beginning. What about the world? What are the people like in the world you live in? To be trusted, or to be feared? On a path of learning and progress, or on a path of self-absorption and destruction? What is the universe bringing your way? When negative events bring supposedly unwelcome change, how do you tend to interpret them? Our assumptions about these things are called life assumptions. Many assumptions operate in our lives, some of which are barely within our awareness. Nonetheless, they have an impact every day.

As an example, one of the eye-opening moments of my life came at the end of a business luncheon with my boss and a well-known training guru. I considered both of them to be intelligent, capable, well-grounded individuals. To some degree, I considered them to be my mentors. We talked of many things. Toward the end of lunch, we began to talk about the purpose of life and the span and structure of same (typical business lunch?).

I referred to my assumption of continuous learning and relationship in the after-life, and mused about what it would be like to live and learn and be in relationship forever with those we love. Their reactions startled me. They emphatically stated that they did not believe in an afterlife. That when we die, that was the end of it. I was taken aback. Up until then, I suppose I thought everyone conceived of an "ever-after", and lived their life accordingly. Because of my life assumptions, my trust in their mentorship wavered from that moment, and wisely so, as it turned out.

We live our life and work our relationships according to our life assumptions. They influence our happiness, our accomplishments, and the quality of our relationships. It has been said that our progress in life is largely determined by the speed with which we discard false notions.

Some of my current empowering life assumptions (things I hold to be true):

1. We will live forever, as individuals.

2. We have and will always have the inviolate power to make choices.

3. I am the sum of my decisions.

4. We are an eternal community.

5. We are responsible to care for the less fortunate.

6. Men are that they might have joy.

7. The earth is a huge and integrated heuristic (self-learning/teaching) device. Each of us is given no more stress (or opportunity) than we can handle.

8. All knowledge prepares us to receive greater knowledge.

9. Our family structure and relationships can be forever.

10. There must be and there will continue to be an opposition in all things— we must experience the bitter to fully appreciate the sweet.

11. We are here on this planet for two reasons: to gain knowledge, (wisdom, intelligence, insight, and practical experience)...and to develop relationships of love and trust. Everything else is fluff.

12. Life's greatest personal growth and joy come as we serve others—to ease other's burdens and to make others happier, more hopeful, and more at peace.

13. Our role in interacting with others is to make bad men good, good men better, and all people happier.

14. All have at least one talent. As we nurture it and share it, we will be given more talents. Each must find and pursue a passion. This is one of the happiness drivers. For some, one passion suffices for the rest of their life. For others, they will have multiple passions. This could be art, music, cooking, volunteer work, teaching, sports participation and coaching, you name it.

15. The difference between good and great is about 3%.

I have many more assumptions. Numbers 5,6,7,8,10,11 and 16 serve me especially well in times of change.

I am not asking you to agree, disagree or judge my assumptions. I am asking you to be aware of your own assumptions and to employ them to enhance your change resilience.

APPLICATION
Employ this principle to benefit you and those you love

Life assumptions lead to (roughly in sequence) outlook, attitudes, actions, habits, and some say "destiny."

One of my life assumptions came from my birth order. I am the oldest sibling, and both of my parents were the oldest of their siblings. I have eight younger brothers and sisters. Said another way, I had changed a lot of diapers by the time I was ten. My diapering responsibilities quickly evolved into many other kinds of responsibilities. I formed a life assumption. This life assumption is expressed in a number of assumptions above, most notably #'s 10 and 13.

What are the life assumptions that you hold? They determine how you view and experience life. They enhance—or limit—your accomplishments and your peace and your happiness. Like Noah's ark, our life assumptions can carry us through the incessant rains of change.

What is life's big picture in your mind? That picture will determine how you treat relationships, your view of money, your endurance in trial, your sense of expectation, your resilience in the face of unexpected change.

What you picture and assume as the way the earth is organized, its ultimate purpose, in other words the overall structure of life before and life after—that mental structure determines your response to change. That structure determines your attitude, the degree of your hope, and the resilience with which you tackle challenge and change.

Many if not most of our life assumptions are given to us by our families and the culture we grow up in. But at a certain point in our life, we have complete freedom to choose our assumptions. Or...we have power to decide their application. We eventually gain the power to live our lives according to any assumptions we choose. Our thoughts are limited by our experience, to be sure, but within our experience, we can make assumptions and live accordingly.

For example, is life on your side, or is life against you? Are you more apt to ask yourself, what does life owe me, or what do I owe life?

In your mind, is life "nasty, brutish and short," to quote the philosopher Hobbes, or is life "a veil of soul-making," to quote the poet Keats? When you move into a new town, what are your expectations? The people living in that town will turn out just like the people in your mind.

What are the life assumptions that you hold and magnify? They will determine how you view and experience life. They will enhance or limit your personal change resilience.

Some of the most basic life assumptions have to do with the degree to which we believe we have control over the events of our lives. One life-structure model is called the Origin/Pawn Model.

This model posits that we all have a basic notion of how much control we have over our lives. All of us see ourselves at different points on a continuum. At one end, we see ourselves as being the origin of our circumstances and the cause of things we make happen. At the other end, we see ourselves as just being a pawn (like on a chessboard), with things happening to us, and we having no control. Where we see ourselves on the continuum determines how proactively we react to change.

We live our lives according to our chosen assumptions. Our thoughts are limited by our experience, to be sure, but within our experience, we can make assumptions and live accordingly.

We should always be looking for new assumptions to be revealed. Thus we grow. If we allow our mind to be stretched by a new idea, it will never regain its original shape.

The Wisdom of K. Hieronymus

We have not chosen here to identify and deal with "negative" life assumptions—many followers of Freud, and other smart people have mined that vein of inert metal, and their books are easy to find, should you desire. While it is true that most of us carry the baggage of life assumptions that are negative or disempowering, we build personal change resilience by focusing on the opposite. We crowd out the negative with positive, just as the best way to prevent weeds in a lawn is to cultivate a thick, lush, healthy carpet of grass (no room for weeds).

So… as you become aware of negative, limiting, blaming, disempowering assumptions, briefly acknowledge their presence, but then focus on magnifying your positive, empowering life assumptions. This will forestall, eclipse, and neutralize the negative.

Cursing gravity is popular these days—don't do it. The gravity of your life is here to stay. Accept it and work within it. We all have limitations, within and without.

Be aware of negative assumptions, and perhaps their origin—there is always a reason and an origin. If knowing the origin (neither as an excuse, nor as a condemnation of self or other, just insight) helps you understand it and let go of it, fine, but do not permit the shadows of negativity to hover over you.

On the flip side, search for and adopt new, empowering assumptions. Be open to discovering new strengths.

LIFE TOOLS™
Use consistently until they become your tools for life

1.   Be honest with yourself regarding where you stand on the three basic life assumptions:

   •   The degree of control you think you have over the events of your life.

   •   The extent to which you believe the events in your life are random, or are designed to "teach" you.

   •   The extent to which you think life is designed to be a plan of happiness, or a plan of suffering.

2.   Place a mark on the continuums below. Where do you see yourself?

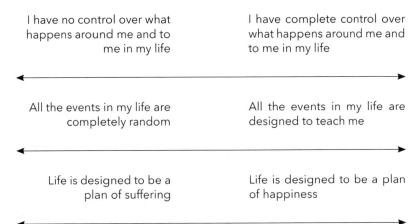

I have no control over what happens around me and to me in my life

I have complete control over what happens around me and to me in my life

All the events in my life are completely random

All the events in my life are designed to teach me

Life is designed to be a plan of suffering

Life is designed to be a plan of happiness

3.   List your current life assumptions: How do you think life works? What happens before and after this life? What is your responsibility to other people? What is really going on? Look at the example list above for ideas. List at least 10.

4.   Write two paragraphs to dig deeper into the Origin/Pawn model as you see it applying to yourself. First, write a candid paragraph describing your life assumptions about how much control you think you have over your life. Be open and complete. To what extent do you see yourself as an origin; to what extent do you see yourself as a pawn?

5.   Then write another paragraph describing the implications of this view in your life day to day, in the last few weeks.

6.   Take steps to "own" your life assumptions. In a trusted, safe group state one of your life assumptions. The group's reaction does not matter. Do not take anything personally. The simple act of "owning who you are," publicly, will be empowering and clarifying to you—not without risk, but empowering. If you need words, just start out, "I believe the way life works is..." The words will come.

7.   Go to someone you admire. Explain the concept of empowering life assumptions. Tell them why you have decided to talk to them. Then ask them what their life assumptions are. Write them down. Read them back and verify that you got it correctly. Incorporate this wisdom into your life

TRAPS

Don't get stuck in the past. Many of our life assumptions come from "tender places," Some might not be pretty. A few might not be empowering. Just take them as they are. Be aware of their boundaries and use them as stepping-stones.

What to do if you cannot identify many or any nourishing life assumptions? You need to start hanging out with different people!

As always, beware the distractions of everyday life. Don't get lost in "the thick of thin things."

PERPETUAL ENCOURAGEMENT

Know that change is a process, a journey with many paths and roads and resting (refreshment) places. You may not know where the next step will lead. The important thing is to just keep on walking.

Know that opportunities often come in disguise. Remember the old saying— "I prayed for patience, and God sent me trials, and through them, I learned patience.

Get into action, even if small. Procrastinate procrastination. For example, if you are worried about your finances, talk to someone who has more training or experience than you. Or read an article in a financial magazine. If you are worried about being out of shape, go for a walk. If you are worried about a family member, call or text or send an email or gift. Move.

APPENDIX

Wordsworth's poem, *"Ode: Intimations of Immortality from Recollections of Early Childhood"* describes one of his life assumptions—

> *"Our birth is but a sleep and a forgetting.*
>
> *The soul that rises with us, our life's star,*
>
> *hath had elsewhere its setting, and cometh from afar:*
>
> *not in entire forgetfulness, and not in utter nakedness,*
>
> *but trailing clouds of glory do we come from God, who is our home."*

You can glean other empowering life assumptions from reading the great literature of notable thinkers and authors.

SUMMARY

1.   Empowering life assumptions are your current nourishing beliefs about how life works and what you can expect from life.

2.   The life assumptions that you hold and magnify will determine how you view and experience life. They will enhance or limit your accomplishments and your peace and your happiness.

3.   Identify your empowering life assumptions.

4.   Post them where you will see them often.

5.   Do not entertain negative life assumptions.

PRINCIPLE 3:

Embrace The Law Of The Harvest

What you sow, you will reap. What you plant, you will harvest. For good or ill. The law of the harvest is a mathematical, statistical law, an immutable law of the universe. Inputs produce outputs, after their kind. What you send forth will come back to you, multiplied. Seeds sown are seeds grown. Take care to sow only what you want to reap.

SONGLINE
Learn to navigate the wilderness of change

When you hold a seed packet in your hand, you see a picture of what the seed will become. Plant the seed, and it brings forth in its likeness. What is less obvious is that thoughts, actions and intentions are like seeds—when planted, they also bring forth in their likeness. Often it is immediate. Or sometimes the seed-harvest skips generations; our progeny benefit.

I came of age in the 60's, but this will not be the normal 60's story, as I was not only there, but I also remember that I was there—if you get my drift. Instead, this story is about a true counterculture that too few experience.

In the winter of 1967, I was home from New York City, home from college on holiday break. A good friend asked me if I would drive her from Boise, Idaho to Provo, Utah, a distance of about 250 miles.

I readily agreed, although probably for the wrong reason (I wanted to meet her roommate, whose picture I had seen some months earlier, enclosed in a letter to my Boise friend—a Virginia girl, and intriguingly attractive. As it turned out, I married the Virginia girl, and 38 years later, we still enjoy spending time together, but I digress).

To return to our instructive tale, we had traveled in her (ancient) car for about 2 hours through the cold and sparse Idaho winter landscape, when the car began to lose power and the engine produced a rhythmic sound like a metal bar tapping against a metal door. Being the man in the car (all of 18 years old), I knew that I was responsible to make it right. Even though I knew a lot about how to survive in the wilderness, should we have to encamp for the night, but next to nothing about automobiles.

We pulled into the nearest town, which happened to be Jerome, Idaho, and found the service station nearest to the highway. Back in those days almost every gas station had an active garage with one or more mechanics. This one was no exception.

I explained the symptoms to the mechanic. He started to fill out the paperwork, and when he heard my name, he said, "Are you Hal Walker's son?". I knew the correct answer was "yes", and it turns out that is also the accurate answer. I have been his son all my life. When I gave my response, he stopped filling out the paperwork and disappeared.

About one hour later he returned and told me the car was repaired—it had been a loose connector rod. I asked him how much it was. He said it was free. I accepted gratefully. I do not know what my father ever did for him, but this is just one of many instances like this. The seed had skipped a generation and born fruit. The car performed perfectly the rest of the journey.

This experience was for me one of those eye-opening life mini-lessons, administered on the outskirts of a very small town, on a very cold night, in a very remote and mostly forgotten corner of the world.

This was proof to me that the law of the harvest is a mathematical, statistical law, an immutable law of the universe: what we sew, we reap. In this case, the seed had been planted years earlier, by an act of service I am sure, because that was what was given back to me.

The life mini-lesson to me was: Embrace the law of the harvest. Sow good seeds, for what you sow, you or someone will eventually reap. The harvest will look a lot like what was planted.

As I have shared this concept with others, I have been taught (gained wisdom) and learned other instances of seed planters.

Wisdom: often we must prepare ourselves to effectively planters of seeds—that's why doctors, architects etc. go to school so long, right? In fact, we are always preparing to be more effective at planting seeds, if we are willing to listen. In your mind, is formal education, some other consistent, structured preparation for the purpose of preparing us to be efficacious seed planters, or simply to "make a living"?

Preparation is one of the things that must be done on faith. It is like building a "spec" house. You must have confidence that if you build it, they will come. You will eventually enjoy a great feeling of satisfaction for having been able to add to someone else's life.

Before you plant seeds, sometimes the land has to be cleared. Every farmer knows this. And the clearing may be violent. The plow violently parts the crust of the land, and turns it over onto itself, exposing the underside (often more fertile). Or, the fire burns off the old stubble or brush, to add nutrients back to the land. Old forms and comforts are broken up. Once-secure jobs disappear. Change happens. Relationships founder, then break apart on the rocks of indifference or infidelity.

All good news—there is a new clear place. Time to plant! Time to turn bad times into good times.

In summary, the law of the harvest really works. What you send out, comes back to you, multiplied. It often comes back unexpectedly, at just the right time, at the time of your need. This principle works unless you do it or the sole purpose of receiving a reward. When you give, give it away, then forget about it. Move on to further service.

APPLICATION
Employ this principle to benefit you and those you love

Doing begets doing; service begets service. As we love others, they love us. As we do good to others, they (or someone) will do good to us. It is mathematical. "Count" on it.

We plant seeds through thoughts and actions. We can plant seeds in our own hearts, or in other's hearts.

Seeds can be planted anywhere, but some soil is more fertile than others. We sometimes cannot know ahead of time how fertile. We must just plant, and await the result in peace.

In other words, not all seeds take hold. Planting seeds to add beauty and "vespers" to ours or others lives is like taking good photos: experienced photographers say you have to take a lot of bad photos to end up with something worth framing.

If you plant seeds expecting immediate "frame-ready" results, you may end up disappointed. Some take time to grow; some die immediately. And some results will be invisible to you, perhaps for a long, long time. Still, do not hesitate to plant. Using all the hope and energy you can muster, using the best techniques and approaches that you know: plant, and await the result in patience and peace. And be satisfied with what may seem a low yield ratio.

Consciously plant seeds in the lives of others—this can be those you care about, or perfect strangers...become more aware of the seeds you may be planting through your example or interaction. Be conscious that you are always planting seeds. Every day of your life. Some are conscious; some are not.

Planting seeds in hearts is the most sure path to the harvest. In the experience described above, the seed had been planted by my father's action. An act of service, to be exact. The seed was planted in the heart of a skilled mechanic.

Sometimes we plant seeds in our own hearts. We plant these seeds by thoughts. We do this by exposing ourselves to new thoughts, and by also entertaining the thoughts that "come into our heads".

We must be willing to allow and entertain seeds of thought—a seed of hope, a seed of forgiveness, a seed of letting go, a seed of (new) interpretation, a seed of determination. If we allow the seed to take root and grow, in short order we reap the benefit.

Caution— short order may take years. This is where faith comes in. Faith creates staying power.

The Wisdom of K. Hieronymus

When challenging times of change are upon us, having been a planter in prior times helps in three ways:

First, seeds planted during times of prosperity may come to fruition when most needed, like the mechanic's favor in my time of need, or like money "saved for a rainy day".

Second, if we are in the habit of planting good seeds, we forget our own troubles and redirect our energy to supporting those less fortunate. Everyone wins. We take our mind off our own "troubles", and the seeds planted help someone else (and may come to fruition, perhaps soon, to help us).

Instead of behaving like a victim, we behave like a planter. Harvest always ensues.

In all cases— first, remember that a seed is never fully planted until you let go of it. Let go and await the result in peace—do not pull up the plant to inspect the roots! Or, if the seed is being planted in yourself, let the seed fully land. Absorb it, "taste it", continue to water it. Examine all sides of it. Repeat it out loud to feel the sound of it. Repeat it silently. Let it echo in your mind.

Second, rejoice in the fruit. Savor the feeling of completion. Be grateful.

This principle applies to so many circumstances: to every spouse who is patient with their spouse's weakness, to every mother who struggles with an overactive child, to every teacher who stands day after day in front of a sleepy-eyed swamp of faces.

In all these endeavors, motive is everything, or rather, it must be nothing. Service must be done with no thought of reward or recognition. It must be given as an offering or a gift, not as an investment or exchange. No strings attached. Only when we let go of the seed can the seed truly be planted.

Opportunities to plant are abundant. Disguised as opportunities to encourage or share. As opportunities to praise. To be attentive. To carry on when you are tired. Opportunities to be there at the 12th son's Cub Scout Pinewood Derby, for example, or at the birth of the new child. Opportunities to give precious gifts, such as, for example, your time. Get in the habit of noticing opportunities. Then you will see the opportunity for good times during bad times.

In practical terms, watch the TV that you watch, be careful who you hang out with. Listen only to uplifting music. What is being planted in your mind and heart will come to fruition. Pick the seed; pick the harvest.

LIFE TOOLS™
Use consistently until they become your tools for life

Do one or more of the following to gain skill in this principle.

1. Make a list of 8 or 10 people that you know. Pick one person on the list who is undergoing a difficult change. Make opportunity to do something helpful or encouraging for that person. It may just be a kind word.

2. Plant new seeds in your own heart/mind. Focus on a change that is challenging you, then ask a trusted person, whether face to face, voice to voice, or electronically, what you should do. An alternate way is "imaginary conversation"— with a trusted person who is not now accessible. Have a dialogue with them—ask them, "What do you think about _____ ?" Then listen.

3. Take time to look at a magazine(s) or book(s), maybe one in your house or on the shelves of a local bookstore. Thumb through the magazine and find an example of someone planting a seed in their own or another's heart. Think if there is any parallel to your situation—either a place in your heart or a need in the heart of another. Is there a possible action that comes to mind? Act now.

4.   This task is longer term: plant a seed of a plant that grows in your climate. Put a person's name on a piece of paper and place it in the pot or ground. As you nourish the plant and watch its progress, notice thoughts that come to mind about the needs of that person. Take action as appropriate. Notice what comes back to you. If you are in a hurry, obtain a plant, and nourish that.

5.   Send an anonymous gift to someone you know, perhaps someone going through a challenging change. The gift can be money, or any other item.

6.   Obtain six index cards. Go to the bookstore and read a quotes book. Find six quotes that you find encouraging or edifying. Write each one down on one of the cards. Post the cards where you will see them about once a day. Do this for a week. Notice what happens and tell someone else about it.

7.   Increase the possibility of good times by creating a clearing (see definition above). Change itself may have already created a clearing in your life, or you may need to cheerfully let that happen. Either way, the opportunity is for something new to be planted—by you or someone else.

     Create clearings by things such as: discarding things that you no longer need (release to the universe), ending a relationship that is no longer to your benefit, giving away the clunker, etc.

8.   Do something that is "not your job". This may be in the realm of doing something "nice" for someone else—in fact, do 5 things that are not your job—at home, work, or volunteer settings. Do this in secret if possible.

TRAPS

Avoid the temptation to expect an immediate, discernible return on every seed you plant. A seed isn't fully planted until you fully let go of it. Plant, then forget.

Don't let shyness stop you, and don't procrastinate. If you feel the barest inclination to encourage or compliment another, for example, act immediately.

PERPETUAL ENCOURAGEMENT

Change energy rule of thumb—try new things twice before you give up.

Awkwardness and potential embarrassment are part of the process of personal change.

Realize that your capacity to live this principle will increase as you work to live the principle. Work increases personal capacity.

APPENDIX

Some quotes in this arena:

"You reap what you sow." - Anonymous

"Whatsoever a man soweth, that shall he also reap." - Christian Bible

"What goes around, comes around." - Redneck Bobby

"He that sows sparingly, shall also reap sparingly, so that if [a people] want a plentiful harvest, they will do well to be at the place of labor in good season in the morning, bringing all necessary tools." - **Joseph Smith**

"One of life's most sublime experiences is to secretly do something nice for someone else, and then be found out by accident." - **Ronald Ross**, former friend and colleague

"Give, and it shall be given unto you; good measure, pressed down, and shaken together, and running over, shall men give into your bosom. For with the same measure that ye give withal shall it be measured to you again." - Christian Bible

SUMMARY

1. What you sow, you will reap. What you invest, you will harvest. What you send forth will come back to you, multiplied. For good or ill.

2. Be sure to plant only what you want to reap.

3. We plant seeds through thoughts and actions.

4. We can plant seeds in our own hearts, or in other's hearts. Planting seeds in hearts is the most effective method.

5. Sometimes the seed produces quickly; sometimes we must nurture for a time before fruition. Patience and persistence are as important as the planting.

6. The harvest often comes back unexpectedly, at just the right time, at the time of need.

7. This principle works unless you follow it for the sole purpose of receiving a reward. Give it away, then forget about it. Selfless service is the prime imperative.

8. Before you plant seeds, sometimes the "land" has to be cleared. And the clearing may be violent. Old forms and comforts must be broken up. All good news—there is a new clear place. Time to plant! Time to turn bad times into good times.

PRINCIPLE 4:

Cultivate Positive Stress

Positive stress is the stress caused by the big change, the big goal, the audacious invitation, the big stretch, the one you are not quite sure you can meet or achieve. Or positive stress is caused by a hefty accumulation of smaller, moderate changes and challenges. Learn to cultivate, embrace and harness the power of stress so it becomes your friend and ally in times of change.

SONGLINE
Learn to navigate the wilderness of change

Change creates stress. Stress can have either a negative or a positive impact. Negative stress is the stress associated with worry, with fear, with trying to control the rate of change, trying to do too much too fast, or holding yourself responsible for things that are not your responsibilities.

Positive stress is different. This is the stress associated with growth, or "growth stress" (G-stress). G-stress increases your resilience in the face of change. It stems from life's benevolent opposition, which makes you stronger.

For example, the resistance employed in strength training to make your muscles stronger, or the strength that comes from engaging with strong, not weak "opponents," is a common type of G-stress. It creates the toughness and prowess that come from "playing in a tough conference."

G-stress is the stress that creates energy that generates excitement that engenders permanent personal power. G-stress is stress that is optimal and positive. It is the opposite, positive twin of Dis-tress (D-stress). Like a space explorer trekking on a planet with a higher gravity, as you apply more G's to your life, you grow stronger.

G-stress is the creative tension just before the breakthrough, the nervousness or gut-squeezing panic at the prospect of the big speech or the high dive.

Change always creates the opportunity for this positive type of stress.

In the 60's, my life changed dramatically, and G-stress asserted its positive power, because of three decisions I made.

One change came in the Spring of my sophomore year, as I sat in typing class staring out the window at the reddish oval cinder track two stories below. The announcement had just blasted over the public address system that track team tryouts were to commence that afternoon after school. I felt an urge to join in. I was nervous, fearing the pain, the challenge, the potential embarrassment if I failed to do well. I wrestled all period and learned very little about touch typing.

Hours later, I signed up. I did not do so well that first season. But I worked hard (G-stress) and found my sport. In the Fall of that year, I earned my varsity letter as a member of the cross-country team. The next Spring, I ran the mile and two mile for the track team. I was not a star, but I held my own, and grew in strength and confidence.

The other decision, two years later, was to run for school office. I ran for senior class president. "Win With Walker" was the slogan. Walker did not win, but it was an experience that created other opportunities. And at least I had the "courage to join the race."

This led to an opportunity. Our high school had not had a chapter of the National Honor Society for a number of years. One of the teachers decided it was time to start it up again. She managed to get most of us "scholars" into a room, and explained that the first step was to elect a president. In a closed ballot vote (piece of paper). This time we did Win With Walker. Taking on this new challenge created stress but also taught leadership lessons that I apply to this day.

A few weeks later, my availability established, I was asked to be editor of our high

The Wisdom of K. Hieronymus

One thing that may feel somewhat like stress, but is not really, is guilt. Guilt comes from deciding to not do something we know we ought to do, or from choosing to do something that we know we ought not to do. Learn to harness and exploit guilt: use it to jumpstart G-stress action.

An acquaintance of mine once had a car that needed to be push-started. Therefore, she always parked her car at the top of a hill, for a gravity-assisted push. Guilt parks your "change wagon" at the top of the hill. Use it to give yourself a little push into action, and you are off and running.

To summarize, guilt can be a great motivator. It can be a great jump-starter. But left in place too long, it becomes an action inhibitor. It creates D-stress and grudging-compliance behavior, not creative-growthful behavior.

school's new literary magazine, again a first in many years for our school. I decided to say yes. My life changed.

My relationship with my peers changed. In the ensuing months, I benefited from the stress and growth that came from judging, editing, and publishing my peers' work.

"No" is also an acceptable answer in the face of opportunity. Intelligent management of G-stress produces power "in the negative." Shortly after taking on the literary magazine, I was asked to take on a responsible (and lucrative) position in a local grocery chain. I was also recruited for the debate team. Through my parents' and other adults' wisdom, after wrestling with the decisions, I said "no" to both these opportunities. Thus I avoided D-stress by not over-extending myself, as must we all if G-stress is to serve us.

Taking full advantage of the potential of G-stress requires answering the question: when the red flag of "danger" whips in the wind, will you gird up your loins and courageously run toward it, or will you run the other way or pretend you do not see it? Will you stand up and face it, or will you retreat and hide?

APPLICATION
Employ this principle to benefit you and those you love

Change drives the opportunity for response. Said another way, change drives the opportunity to make commitments. There are two kinds of commitments, or goals—maintenance goals, and stretch goals.

Maintenance goals help you consolidate gains—they keep things in order and maintain the base of your life.

This includes things such as changing the oil in the car, regularly saying "I love you" to your spouse, making sure the rent is paid or there is milk in the fridge, or keeping the flower beds weeded and fertilized. Setting maintenance goals is an important life activity, and when the maintenance goals don't work out, you learn and reset. If the weather changes and one crop fails, you do your research and plant another, perhaps different.

Stretch goals drive you to do things you might never have done before, and you are not sure you can accomplish—they keep you ahead of change; they are literally a stretch, but you intend to accomplish them. These are things such as losing 40 pounds in five months, contacting your parents without fail every week, selling more in one month than you ever sold before, completing a block of education, clearing out and planting a whole new flower bed with flowers you have never tried before—before the frozen breath of winter stops further progress. Stretch goals are the main source of G-stress.

Stretch goals can evolve into valuable maintenance goals. For example, an exercise habit, difficult at first, can morph into a habit that becomes part of who you are. The speed at which this happens is one measure of how quickly you are developing change resilience.

Tremors of fear can be a sign to you that you are about to experience a positive shift to more G-stress opportunities. In other words, fear can be a positive sign of incipient progress.

When you understand this, you can courageously face and embrace the unexpected challenges that a change of life throws your way. When the car breaks down, when job loss challenges your enthusiasm, when the value of your life savings suddenly evaporates, then is the time to harness the power of G-stress.

In sum, two responses to changes can happen in our lives, which will drive either D-stress, or G-stress: resistance and retreat, or anticipation and embrace.

The most important G-stress skill is learning to set successive, progressive goals. This enables strength to build upon strength for steps up the staircase of accomplishment. Each goal fulfillment leads to a higher goal, a progressive journey of stretch.

A week is the perfect microcosm of a life. Most weeks contain in some combination, all the opportunity elements of a month or a year—work time, play time, worship time. Set weekly targets that build to monthly and yearly targets.

Make time to review where you are in your goal achievement. Every day, or even several times a day, evaluate how you are spending your time. The reminder system that is described in the lead-in chapter is a perfect example of a mechanism to aid this practice.

Another G-stress skill is learning when and how to rest. If the bow is left tightly strung all the time, it loses its spring. Given rest, it regains and retains resilience. In competitive cycling, there is a phenomenon known as "overtraining." This occurs when a cyclist engages in intense workouts, day after day after day. The body does not have time to recover. The cells do not rejuvenate and grow stronger. Stamina actually decreases. Sickness is likely. The trick is to stay just at the edge of the stress and growth threshold, in the G-stress zone.

Often, a "G-stress excursion" hits a wall at some point. This is the point of near-breakthrough, the point when you are more tired, more stressed than ever before in this arena, the point where many give up.

Instead of giving up, resist the temptation to stop. You may be just at the edge of standing on a new platform of strength. Continue movement.

That said, there will be times when you should give up, times when your intuition is accurately saying, "Wrong Path." As you gain more experience in the active zone of G-stress, you will develop discernment and sense when to back off.

Cultivating G-stress causes personal growth that creates strength and resilience in the face of change and uses the energy of change to the advantage of yourself and those you care about.

When I was in my middle teens, I had an all-summer job laying sprinkler pipe in the potato fields of southern Idaho. It was extremely difficult work. Each pipe weighed 40 pounds, each line was a quarter mile (33 pipes) long, each pipe had to be carried 40 feet, many pipes were filled with water at first, the vegetation tugged at my ankles, the sun was hot, or the rain and wind were cold, the gnats swarmed and bit at my ears, eyes, and nose and flew into my mouth, and the terrain was at times uneven. But the hardest part was that the line had to be laid perfectly straight, or the space between sprinklers, day to day, would be uneven and the crops would receive either too much or little water in spots. And the owner paid close attention. At first I was not very good at keeping things in line.

Then I learned to fix my eye on a far landmark, way beyond the field. I laid each pipe pointing at the landmark. When I got to the end of the line of pipe, I looked back, and it was perfectly straight.

Fixing on the "North Star," as it were, at the far horizon kept the day's effort in perfect alignment.

LIFE TOOLS™
Use consistently until they become your tools for life

1. Make a list of six changes that have recently come into your life, whether caused by you, by others, or by circumstances. Which ones caused the most stress? Now analyze: Was the effect D-stress, or was it G-stress? Is there an opportunity to change D-stress into G-stress? Write a few sentences about both these questions.

2. Look back into your history, and you will see a few times of enormous stress. Normally these involve a change of some kind. Write a few sentences describing one that you believe resulted in personal growth.

3. Set five maintenance goals. Set two stretch goals. Remember that goals need to be SMAC:

   S= Specific

   M= Measurable

   A= Achievable

   C= Compatible with your highest priorities

   Share these goals with someone you trust.

4. Ask two people—what do you think is the next area of growth for me? How am I going to take full advantage of the opportunities for that? What could I do differently? Set a really big goal in that area, one that makes you nervous. Start.

5. What thing is causing the most stress in your life right now? How could you turn this into G-stress? Send an email or postcard to yourself, giving yourself advice in this area. Pretend you are sending it to a close friend whom you greatly love.

TRAPS

1. Avoid the trap of over-achievement. If you find yourself feeling that you never do enough, or that what you do is never good enough, you might be falling victim to this trap. Step back, take a deep physical and emotional breath, and reevaluate. Be open to concluding that what you have already done is just fine.

2. Beware the distractions of everyday life. Don't get lost in the thick of thin things.

PERPETUAL ENCOURAGEMENT

At G-stress opportunities, do not run the other way. Face them head-on and consciously decide. Remember what William J. Lock said, "Half the unhappiness in life comes from people being afraid to go straight at things."

As a way to reframe the challenge of change: if you did not cause a change that is making your life difficult, pretend you did—why would you have done this?

Take to heart the Chinese proverb: "When the winds of change blow, some build walls; others build windmills."

Remember: Persistent resistance to change brings atrophy and death. Constant openness to change (making the most of it) brings growth and life.

Know that you are unique. Change and consequent G-stress can drive your uniqueness. Be willing to consider the possibility that you have a mission to fulfill, a contribution to make, that is different from that of every other person on the planet. Know that as you step out into your spotless future, the means will appear to help you carry out your unique contribution.

Get into action, even if small. Procrastinate procrastination. For example, if you are worried about your finances, take time to read an article in a financial magazine. If you are exhausted, take a break. Or a nap.

APPENDIX

"Life is either a daring adventure or nothing. Security does not exist in nature, nor do the children of men as a whole experience it. Avoiding danger is no safer in the long run than exposure." - **Helen Keller**

"That which we persist in doing becomes easier, not that the task itself has become easier, but that our ability to perform it has improved." - **Ralph Waldo Emerson**

"What does not kill me makes me stronger." - **Friedrich Nietzsche**

SUMMARY

1. Change creates stress.

2. Stress can have either a negative or a positive impact. Negative stress is the stress associated with worry, with fear, with trying to control.

3. Positive stress is the stress that stimulates growth. Like the resistance employed in strength training, it stems from life's opposition, and it makes you stronger.

4. Positive stress can be created by setting goals.

5. There are two kinds of goals—stretch goals, and maintenance goals. Stretch goals are difficult; maintenance goals are not hard but are sometimes hard to maintain with consistency. Both are important to building change resilience.

6. Fear often occurs in the face of the stress of change. It is sometimes a sign that you should retreat; it is often a sign that you are about to approach something very important.

7. Pushing through stress brings growth.

8. Grow stronger faster by facing G-stress head on.

PRINCIPLE 5:

Reframe Bad/Good

Reframe your definition of what is bad and what is good. Look at the bigger picture. Look for the pattern and the progress within the pattern. Look to change as an opportunity to build new strength and greater change resilience. Remember the words of Rudyard Kipling— "Meet with triumph and disaster, and treat those two imposters just the same."

SONGLINE

Learn to navigate the wilderness of change

He knew one speed, one trick, one move. Move forward. Push hard. If you get stuck, exert more effort. As **Leonardo da Vinci** asserted—Every obstacle yields to stern resolve. But in this case, this strategy was the road to slow and thirsty death.

I am referring to the turtle that I found stuck in the wire fence that surrounds our property, stuck so solidly that I could not tug him free—wire cutters were necessary. Who knows what was in his turtle brain, but he had obviously set out on a turtle adventure, making tracks across the top of the rocky hill where our house is situated. The wire fence would have been his death place, had I not been working in that section and spotted him.

He was a water turtle, judging by the dark mud stains, and also a well-traveled turtle, judging by all the scrapes and gouges in his carapace. And now he was a saved turtle.

His consternation must have continued, as I filled a shallow pan with water, placed him in it, cut off a few slices of banana, and placed a large blue recycling bin over the whole, to keep him around for awhile to show to the kids (all in their 20's and 30's, but animal lovers to the core) before setting him free. And also for his protection from the ravenous cats that prowl our property.

From the turtle's perspective, things had now gone from bad to worse. Disaster impended. What must he have thought? Did he ask himself what the blue, impenetrable expanse was that now hemmed him in? Here was water, here was food (maybe—though a type of soft, smelly food he had never experienced before—he would have preferred a nice, squishy earthworm), but where was freedom? Where were the good old days of sauntering through his care-free turtle life? Did he despair? Did he curse the fates? Was he tempted to renounce turtle polytheism? Did he rant at his captor, when he should have rejoiced in his deliverer?

After most of the kids had seen and ooh-ahhed at the specimen, sometime during the night, said turtle pushed under the blue barrier and I suppose made it to the stream that runs close by. So maybe his push-ahead resolve was the right approach after all. But not without the "divine intervention" of my wire cutters.

My point here is both about approach and about perspective. Had our turtle been a thinking turtle (I have no evidence that he was not), he might have mightily despaired at his stuck-ness. He might have engaged in any number of superstitious remedies, incantations, and invectives. He might have wondered why he was being punished.

The parallels to our situations are obvious. From time to time, unexpected change strikes: we become the turtle stuck in the fence. We use our tried and proven strategies. They do not work. We despair and rant.

We forget to remember how those things that at one time in our life we thought were disasters were really insignificant. So what if we did not receive the lead role in the high school play? So what if we missed the winning shot. So what if when the time came to pop the question, Mary Lou said no. Quite frankly, no one remembers the school play nor the significance of the game. And Mary Lou turned out to be...(you know the rest of the story).

Yes, I know, some things really did turn out to be bad. You have evidence. This is an opportunity. Remember the building of your character?

Let's look at a simple example, a common enough change, that is surely seen as negative but may not necessarily be: a beloved companion of decades dies. Grief and pain are close to overwhelming. But with the help of family and friends, and as years go by, the one left behind acquires an independence of spirit, a space for personal expression, that never would have happened otherwise. Character growth ensues—large caliber change resilience occurs.

APPLICATION
Employ this principle to benefit you and those you love

A friend once said, while teaching a large group of people, "If things are bad, they will get better." And then he paused, gazed compassionately at the audience, and said, "And if things are good, they will get worse."

We all wanted to hear the first sentence, but not the second. Our dream, like most dreams, was that change will always be for the good, that all things will become better and better, bigger and bigger, more and more expansive, more comfortable, easier. We did not want ups and downs. We wanted unbroken upward progress and plateaus of constant well-being.

But real life consists of ups and downs. And sometimes, as with the surfer thrown off the board by an unexpected change in the wave, pressed under water, franti-

 *The Wisdom of K. Hieronymus*

Beware the stack-attack! When change challenges you, you may experience a stack-attack. A stack attack occurs when those potent, painful memory neurons of similar nature, stacked up in our brain, one on top of another, are unleashed by an experience similar to earlier painful experiences. The emotional reactions stored up in these memories "attack" us all at once. This is also sometimes referred to as a panic attack.

The brain is designed this way. This design is often helpful: present stimuli and challenges are often best met by accessing past experience.

Unfortunately, negative emotions and memories from past experiences sometimes take precedence over reason. Present pain triggers the negative energy of past similar pain, and past emotional reactions, logical or not. These then come crowding in, which can be disabling.

Best strategy? Mark Twain's illustration of the cat on the hot stove is helpful: "We should be careful to get out of an experience only the wisdom that is in it, and stop there; lest we be like the cat that sits down on a hot stove lid. She will never sit down on a hot stove lid again—and that is well; but also she will never sit down on a cold one anymore!"

Don't succumb to the cat on the hot stove deception!! Ignore the stack attack and take the logical, not emotional path. Go about your business and see what happens. Schedule a time to attend to it later (if necessary).

cally flailing to establish movement towards air, what may seem down is really up. Suddenly, the water-enclosed surfer bumps into the hard ocean bottom. The realization strikes. What seemed good before is now recognized as bad (ocean floor, not free air). Once realized, the surfer swims with altered direction, and finally breaks through the surface to gulp the oxygen of life. From the experience, the surfer gains skill and deeper appreciation for another day of life.

Like it or not, we are all surfing on life's waves of change. When we take a spill, what appears down is often up. And sometimes "down" supplies the knowledge that leads to "up." We need to keep swimming, even as we hold our breath until the breakthrough comes.

On another occasion, a friend said—again, while teaching a large group whom he knew and loved— "All the painful, trying things that happen to you are designed to build your character." In other words, to make you stronger, more resilient, more compassionate. In a phrase, to literally build our character. He was pointing the inestimable upside of unwanted change.

To say that an experience will be character building is almost a cliché, a joke. People in pain do not appreciate the suggestion. I have had people turn on me in anger when I have offered this way of looking at difficult experience. Nonetheless it is true. I will continue to advocate welcoming all change as part of a larger character-building design.

That said, there are times when what seems good is really bad, like the shiny toy that lasts only hours because of poor construction, or the car that turns out to be more of a cash-drain than a thrill-booster. These things give us opportunity to grow in wisdom and judgment.

Or, there are times when something is genuinely bad, and our lack of attention to the damage being done causes what could have been a mere disaster to become a genuine tragedy.

Our focus here is more on that which may seem immediately bad, yet contains opportunity, and is a proving ground and builder of change resilience.

Remember this Chinese Proverb: "Sāi Wēng Lost his Horse"

Sāi Wēng lived on the border and he raised horses for a living. One day he lost a horse and his neighbor felt sorry for him, but Sāi Wēng didn't care about the horse, because he thought it wasn't a bad thing to lose a horse. After a while the horse returned with another beautiful horse, and the neighbor congratulated him on his good luck. But Sāi Wēng thought that maybe it wasn't a good thing to have this new horse.

His son liked the new horse a lot and often took it riding. One day his son fell off the horse and broke his leg. Because of his broken leg, he couldn't go off to the war, as was expected of all the young men in the area. Most of them died.

This proverb is said when bad luck turns to good, or when good luck turns to bad.

In fact, except for extreme cases, we ultimately are not wise enough to know, from a long-term perspective, what is bad and what is good. We see a small picture. That which we sought and did not find, which seemed a terrific loss at the time, now turns out to be an experience best missed, a blessing by its absence. As **Garth Brooks** sang, "Sometimes I thank God for unanswered prayers".

LIFE TOOLS™
Use consistently until they become your tools for life

1.   Reorder your thinking by using the five badness/goodness questions.

Notice something "bad" that has just happened (or in recent months). Ask yourself:

- Why do I say this is bad (and who else might say it is bad)?

- What flavor of "bad" is it? Refer to the synonyms of "bad" in the appendix and choose the one that best fits, or come up with your own word or expression.

- Has anything similar happened to me in the past, and what was the outcome?

- What are my current emotions, and are they appropriate to the situation?

- What good might come from this? To spark your thinking, you might circle the definitions of "good" that come closest to describing the possibilities. Said another way, what could be some possible long-range advantages of this occurrence?

2.   Reorder your behavior by taking the three reordering steps.

- Look for a "teacher" and get into dialogue. Think of this person as a "trusted advisor"—someone to talk to, preferably someone who has been through something similar. Some say, "When a learner is ready, a teacher appears." Share your experience. Listen to their perspective. (If part of your belief system, you may also use prayer or meditation to gain access to this knowledge). You are looking for advice, and also perspective. You are also looking for someone who will ask you "What do you plan to do next?"

- Take immediate action to counter or respond to a difficult change. For example, if you just received a speeding ticket, write a check and pay the fine as soon as possible. Or, if you are going to fight it, sketch your argument on a piece of paper. If you just received bad numbers on a health checkup, buy a sack of healthy groceries on the way home from the doctor's office.

- Lastly, find someone who has recently suffered in this exact area. Do something to help them, even if it is only to offer an encouraging word.

3. Reorder your present awareness. Write down the thing that is bothering you the most right now. List seven ways something positive might come from this. Go ahead—be silly. Use your God-given imagination. Think both short-term and long-term.

TRAPS

1. Avoid excessive unhealthy food as a distraction from what you should be working on—this means an excess of anything loaded with sugar, fat, salt, or caffeine. Chocolate in moderation is, of course, just fine!

2. Avoid unhealthy "friends" who are dripping with sympathy and quick to cast blame on others. Or who will offer reasons for why life is indeed unfair and irreparably bad. This logic leaves us right where we started, or worse.

PERPETUAL ENCOURAGEMENT

As always, beware the distractions of everyday life. Don't get lost in "the thick of thin things." Rather, jump into the thick of only things that are important to you. Distraction is one of the three thieves of lasting happiness.

"Don't let a burp turn into a blowup."

- **Former client**, a precision machining shop manager in South Georgia

"God moves in a mysterious way
His wonders to perform ...
Ye fearful saints, fresh courage take;
The clouds ye so much dread
Are big with mercy and shall break
In blessings on your head...

His purposes will ripen fast,
Unfolding every hour;
The bud may have a bitter taste,
But sweet will be the flow'r."

- William Cowper, 1774

APPENDIX

The many synonyms for Bad—

Sad, mad, faulty, void, evil, inadequate, defective, faulty, flawed; execrable, lesser, low-grade, mediocre, reprehensible, second-rate, unspeakable; bum, useless, valueless, worthless; inadequate, insufficient, lacking; astray; scurrilous, villainous, deficient, inferior, lousy, off, poor, punk, rotten, substandard, unacceptable, ungodly, unsatisfactory, wanting, wretched, wrong, reprobate, blameworthy

The many synonyms for Good—

Comely, delectable, correct, decorous, proper, seemly; high-minded, noble, principled; commendable, good as gold, the best, creditable, exemplary, legitimate; esteemed, law-abiding, reputable, respected, upstanding, worthy; blameless, clean, guiltless, immaculate, incorruptible, innocent, inoffensive, irreproachable, unobjectionable; lily-white, pure, scrupulous, spotless, uncorrupted, unerring

SUMMARY

1. Changes that seem bad for us are often good for us—we do not see the larger pattern, and need to patiently persist until the benefit reveals itself. Keep moving. Expect relief. Expect breakthrough.

2. Life consists of ups and downs. And in this life, we never arrive and never stop growing so long as we stay engaged. Cherish the good times; learn from and outlast the bad times.

3. Do not fall into the trap of expecting unbroken leisure and happiness (bliss) as the end goal of living. Notice how many retire, then soon die. Treat retirement as the gateway to fresh opportunities.

4. Do not be thrown off your purpose by the "stack attack." Be objective about present challenges, put them into perspective, then move forward.

5. Notice the good that has come from "bad" times. In your present thinking, reframe bad to good. Persist.

6. In rare instances, be ready to recognize that something really is bad, though it may have earlier seemed good. Depart from it.

PRINCIPLE 6:

Pursue Personal Talent

Talent development enlarges change resilience. Create space and opportunity to discover and develop your talents. Know that everyone has at least one talent, and that great joy comes from creatively developing and "giving talents away." Know that to be human is to be creative.

SONGLINE

Learn to navigate the wilderness of change

I was a teenager. It was a singular, never-to-be-forgotten moment. A change-trigger moment. I was sitting in church listening to the sermons. Our church has no paid clergy; talks are given by volunteers. I had never seen this particular volunteer speaker before. He was from a different congregation and was a visiting guest speaker. In the language of change, he was there because our regional ecclesiastical leader had brought a Type IV Change (Unwelcome, Unanticipated) into his life in asking him to address our congregation. He had accepted the challenge.

He was decidedly nervous. He was stumbling, stammering, pausing to fasten on his notes, moving by stops and starts, gulping great gulps of air for seemingly no reason. He confessed his extreme anxiety. His delivery was halting and boring. He confessed he had never given a talk before. It was terribly uncomfortable for me to see an adult in such a fix. And there were a long 15 minutes yet to go. We all cringed, and felt badly for him.

Then suddenly something marvelous happened. He found his voice! He began to speak fluently.

His words fell together in logical and inspiring cadence. We could tell by the shock in his eyes and the amazement on his face that he was as surprised as we were. He remarked about how fun it was to speak in public. He became so voluble that he needed to be reminded when his time was up (more than up, actually).

In that moment he had discovered a talent. I was witness.

I never saw him again, but I have to believe this was a major point of turning in his life. I have to believe that this was not his last talk, and that he continued to improve.

Talent discovery and development opportunity happen all the time. I have come to believe that these happy occasions are as ubiquitous as air. Actually, as ubiquitous as change, and often triggered by change. If you are open, you will be in a continual process of discovering your talents in response to changing needs and circumstances.

Even in the absence of change, new personal talent acquisition is possible and desirable. Proactively taking on the personal quest of talent development is a proactive way to cause, embrace, and transmute the positive energy of change.

The process is simpler than you think. You need to remember only four things: (1) Be active in learning new outlook and skill. (2) Organize yourself to be open and willing to apply the talent. (3) Act, no matter how clumsily at first. (4) Persist.

By doing so you will grow in change resilience and joy.

Some people understand this better than others.

My wife understood it. A quick and sure way to bring a flickering fire into her eye was to say, "I am not creative; I don't have talent." She not only would take exception; she would take a stand. I have seen her do this many times. Her conviction was that it is as inane to say "I don't have a talent for art," for example, as it is to say "I don't have a talent for reading." No one is born able to read. Yet, excepting those with congenital limitations, all who apply themselves to learning to read (a fairly complex task) actually do learn to read.

Her point was—if you can learn to read, you can learn to create—whether painting, cooking, singing, writing, sewing, teaching, gardening. So, by extension, there is no such thing as a "brown thumb," or "not being able to carry a tune in a bucket."

I know there are many who would vehemently dispute this. Fine—if you had said that to my wife, you would have needed to duck quickly.

She set the example by tackling creativity in all manner of venues. She believed that we do not stop creating until the day we die (and according to her belief, not then either).

She proved this to me. She would not accept that I was not creative. She gave me a set of 18×22 painting boards for Christmas one year. She also gave me money to buy acrylic paints, and a book with lessons on painting. I made a brave start—but very tentatively. I learned brush strokes. I learned color combinations. I played around with different strokes and color combinations. I painted a few pictures that looked terrible. Mostly I practiced on heavy paper from an artist's tablet that I purchased (to save money).

After a few weeks she asked me how it was going. I showed her my few attempts, and told her that the other painting boards were untouched, because I did not want to waste them. She disappeared for a few moments, then returned with a handwritten note: "I hereby grant license to Lorin R. Walker to forthwith waste any and all painting boards in his possession." She had dated and signed it.

After laughing at her determination that I discover my freedom to create, I dug in and wasted a lot of painting boards, including a few that other people have asked if they can have, and one painted late in the evening, while on a business trip, that was so thrilling to me that I was unable to sleep for hours. I did not know that color could be made to be so vibrant. I was shocked at my creativity. This and other creative activities have been a continuing source of great enjoyment, and have helped me be resilient in the face of change: no matter how daunting or disconcerting the change event, I always have my creative relaxation.

Through this and other experiences, I have learned that once the creativity bug bites, it does not go away. It keeps biting. Talent development is eternal.

APPLICATION
Employ this principle to benefit you and those you love

Myth: Some are talented; most aren't.

Reality: Everyone has some talent for something.

The truth is, everyone has at least one talent that is ready for use. And everyone has the capacity to develop additional talents.

The payoff? The more highly developed your talents are, the more resilient you are in the midst of change. The more strongly you move in the direction of talent acquisition, the more resilient you are in moving surely through the turbulence of transformation, like the self-contained spinning of a personal gyroscope.

There are six types of talent, and five stages of talent development.

The six types of talent are:

- **Intellectual talent:** your mental processing capability.
- **Social talent:** your capacity to form and grow relationships.
- **Physical talent:** your strength, coordination, endurance, speed, flexibility.
- **Judgment/Wisdom talent:** your intelligence to make positive choices that work as intended. Expressive talent—your ability to convey meaning (through speech, song, physical creation, or writing, for example).
- **Creative talent:** this capacity underlies all your talent. Creativity is the in-

herent capacity and drive to make things that don't exist yet.

The five stages of talent development are:

- **Awareness:** something keeps attracting your attention.

- **Exploration:** you try it on. You scribble. You volunteer. You do something small in an area of interest. You move forward despite awkwardness, fear, or clumsiness.

- **Generation:** you begin to consciously produce in an area of interest. You try a new recipe. You dig in the dirt. You step out, with purpose. You place the blank piece of paper, or art board, or recipe book, or computer screen, squarely in front of your eyes and start creating. You don't worry about whether it is any good or not. You just do it.

The Wisdom of K. Hieronymus

Talent is infinite: there is not a finite number of gifts and talents bestowed at birth. The storehouse is endless, and may be delved into at any point in our existence.

Talents build upon one another. Everything we learn prepares us to learn more—everything we learn lays the foundation to learn something else. Remember the life assumption, "We are eternally perfectible beings"?

Some research has shown that the only difference between one who is highly talented at something and one who is not is 10,000 hours of practice. That translates to being engaged in that activity for half our working hours (1000 hours a year) for ten years. Double that time to 2,000 hours, or full time, for five years. After either 5 or 10 years, you have become a "talented" individual.

- **Polishing:** you refine, tweak, take away, add to, embellish, fix typos and add interesting twists.

- **Communication:** you consider the audience. You find the best way to position, sometimes through trial and error. You connect your creation with the outer world.

Be sure to persevere in taking your talent development through all five stages.

To identify your talent, answer the following:

- What are the things you find yourself repeatedly interested in? What do you most enjoy doing? These could be a clue to talent that you should develop.

- Where are you willing to volunteer your time?

- What are you consistently asked to do? This might point to a personal talent.

- What are the activities that, when you do them, you find yourself losing all track of time?

- What are the activities that, when you do them, you feel good about yourself?

- What are the activities that, when you do them, others feel good about themselves?

- What talents do you most appreciate in others? This could be a clue to where you would be willing to invest energy to develop a personal talent.

Expressing talent requires energy. As long as you are alive, energy is available. Sometimes you direct energy in a negative or destructive fashion. This expression takes on many forms—stubbornness, resistance, sarcasm, etc. these emotions are often in response to change. These negative ways of expressing energy are counterproductive in the times of rapid change that are upon us.

Your opportunity is to take this same energy, currently expressed in a negative way, and turn it to the positive. Energy is being expended either way; why not turn it to your advantage and the advantage of those you love?

When you redirect energy to positive ends, for example, stubbornness becomes determination, resistance becomes logical caution, sarcasm becomes insightful advice, etc.

LIFE TOOLS™

Use consistently until they become your tools for life

1. Examine a Type IV change from Principle One. What talent might this call forth? Take steps to develop it.

2. Identify your "Talent Palette." Make a two-column list. In one column list 5-10 things you are good at, even if you are not the best in the world. When you have finished that list, in a parallel column, make a list of the things you most enjoy doing. This is sometimes a clue to what you are also good at or may become good at. Focus on doing something that is on both lists. Or start where you feel the energy to start. In fact, you may already be working on a talent. Give yourself permission to step up the effort.

3. Surround yourself with creative beauty. From the internet, gather paintings or other visual things (such as designs or photographs) that appeal to you. Go for colorful, cheerful, dramatic, unusual colors and combinations. Create your own personal collection of 20 or so. Make this collection your screensaver on your computer, or make it into a paper collage. Or go to a thrift store or garage sale and purchase something just because you like the way it looks. Set aside time periodically to look at your collection. Notice what this does to your awareness of color and beauty in your surroundings.

4. Announce your talent. In a group setting (two or more people), use words such as, "I have decided that I have a talent (or you may say—I have decided that I am going to take more time to develop my talent) for X. I am going to take time to develop that talent by... (you finish the rest)."

5. Ask five people what they think your main talents are. Then ask yourself which of the talents you think you would enjoy the most. Generate increased personal activity in that area.

6. Think of something that you have always wanted to try, but never quite had the courage to try. Take the first step. Doubt your doubts.

7.   Create an environment for creativity—this can be as little as a corner of a room: like Picasso's garage/studio (Google it).

8.   Sign up for a class in an area of interest (talent) or buy an object or piece of equipment related to the talent. Gear up!

TRAPS

Do not allow yourself to say, "I am not talented."

Do not allow yourself to say, "I am not creative."

PERPETUAL ENCOURAGEMENT

Be courageous. Courage means going forward despite fear, not being free from fear.

Remember that paintings are never finished; they just stop in interesting places.

I have come to believe this is true—I can learn to do anything. Not in this life; there is not enough time. But yes, anything.

Another, simplified, way to describe the true path of talent development, is to (1) identify it, (2) develop it and (3) give it away.

Remember that fear is the great talent-killer. Fear stops us. Fear of what others may think makes us hesitate, maybe forever. Move forward in the face of fear. It will eventually take its proper place beneath our feet.

Let talent flow—sometimes it just happens. When you just let it happen, talent takes over. Even if slightly nurtured, creativity will spontaneously capture our time, your energy, your attention. You will not be able to help yourself. Don't try to stop. Just keep on. The dishes or lawn or email or vacuuming can wait for awhile.

APPENDIX

You've got to sing like you don't need the money
Love like you'll never get hurt
You've got to dance like nobody's watchin'
It's gotta come from the heart
If you want it to work

By **Susanna Clark/Richard Leigh** (as sung by **Kathy Mattea**)

Remember the Change Grid from Principle One: Use Type IV change (unanticipated, unwelcome) as an impetus for talent development.

"That self-doubt is going to come back in," says sports psychologist **Nicole Detling Miller**. "I don't care how mentally tough you are. I don't care how good you are. It will happen. Absolutely, it will happen for everyone." So Miller tells skaters to trust the people who believe they can succeed. Embrace that confidence, she says, from coaches, friends, and family.

Quote from National Public Radio broadcast, February 10, 2010

SUMMARY

1. Know that we all have at least one talent.

2. Developing talents is a proactive way to grow change resilience.

3. To start talent development, surround yourself with creative beauty, or make a list of things you are good at, in your personal opinion, or that you enjoy.

4. Pick one and take time to develop it. One good way to start is to announce in public that you are going to develop "Talent X".

5. Get started and persist.

PRINCIPLE 7:

Feed Your Self-Esteem

Self-esteem is the guardian of self through the storms of change. Self-esteem means holding a positive yet balanced view of yourself, including both strengths and weaknesses, and accepting and embracing all of it. It means to habitually cultivate positive conclusions about yourself and your potential. To constantly look for the good in yourself. To accept the love and approval of others. To allow for and learn from mistakes, missteps, and also successes as part of the growth process.

SONGLINE

Learn to navigate the wilderness of change

Cultivate a positive, realistic self concept and increase your self-esteem.

Self-concept is a private, personal, self-managed picture of and feeling about yourself. It consists of your perceptions about yourself, and also your conclusions and feelings about yourself. This is also sometimes called self- image.

Self-esteem is a positive, yet realistic, self-concept, generated through action, learning, inclusive perspective, and service. Self-esteem is built on acceptance of self as a being-in-progress.

Increasing your self-esteem enhances your change resilience. If you know who you are in the face of confusing or negative messages conveyed to you by the "slings and arrows of outrageous fortune(from **Shakespeare**'s *Hamlet*)," you are able to ignore messages that attack your worth.

You can continue to set goals that are relevant, find ways to accomplish those goals, and not blame others for your perceived failures. You will find a way to diagnose personal lack of motivation or effectiveness, make adjustments, and move forward.

You read about the life assumptions that carry us through times of change, in the chapter called "Magnify Empowering Life Assumptions." Self-esteem assumptions are a special set of life assumptions, comprised of perceptions of, conclusions concerning, and feelings about the self. Two things are at the heart of self-esteem: one is continuing self-knowledge, including "the good, the bad, and the ugly;" the other is knowledge that we are all beings-in-progress.

In the beginning, you generate self-esteem assumptions from a combination of an attitude you brought into the world and the verbal and physical affirmations bestowed by the people who surrounded you.

Perhaps you had a number of positive inputs as I did. Perhaps you had parents who loved and affirmed you.

Many adults who were significant to me told me positive things that stuck with me—"you sing well, you are a fast runner, you are both an athlete and a scholar, you are not a quitter, you write well, I like the way you look me in the eye when I shake your hand," and numerous other things—and my parents were always diligent in relaying to me the spoken praise of others. All these inputs have been a wonderful endowment.

We all receive different inputs, some positive, some negative. As our lives continue to change and evolve, some of these messages become conclusions that stick with us. As we progress in our lives, we gain more power to choose which inputs we will carry with us.

If you did not have the benefit of a large number of positive childhood inputs, then you must learn to fasten onto the ones you do receive, and to create more for yourself.

Over time, you can gain a constancy of self-esteem that can be independent of outer circumstance. You can find ways to turn negative change and happenstance to your advantage, even if only in how you frame your thoughts and feelings about the experiences.

Sometimes there is a mismatch between your self-perception and others' perception of you. Others might have a perception of you that is more positive, and you would do well to adopt their perception, and abandon yours.

I first became aware of the power of discrepancy of personal perception and others' (more positive) perception at the outset of my first job out of graduate school. I knew I was untested, my knowledge shot with holes and without the leavening of experience when I took my first manager of training job in Dallas. But I quickly became aware that those who worked for me thought I was really smart. They looked at my advanced degrees, my experience with well regarded organizations, and concluded I really knew what I was talking about. I knew better.

Over time, I brought my self-perceptions more into line with their perceptions.

I further noticed that my children, in most instances, had very positive views of themselves. One child in particular said at a quiet moment of introspection— "Ah like myself" (He spoke with a Texas accent at the time). I have tried to preserve and nurture this attitude. A worthy lifelong project.

My self-perception became richer as I learned of my heritage. I learned of the great pioneering men and women, my ancestors, who had established the Walker clan in the mountains and valleys of southern Idaho. I learned of the Weeks clan who, in one generation, and amidst death by prairie fire and the trauma of death of multiple children, made their way, one footstep at a time, from Connecticut to the majestic mountains of Utah, and hewed out a living in the green garden spot they established in the shadows of the mountains.

Knowing your heritage and ancestors grounds you. The knowledge of personal, ancient roots anchors you in who you are and can be.

APPLICATION
Employ this principle to benefit you and those you love

Self-concept consists of embracing all of who you are, including the good, the bad, the beautiful, and the ugly. Thus you derive an accurate, complete, and inclusive self-concept. As a malleable, teachable, constantly improving being, you can learn from it all and put it all to good use.

As stated before, self-esteem is composed of realistic yet positive and hopeful conclusions and feelings about the self. Embracing those conclusions is a lifelong quest that must continue until the leaven of self-esteem is baked into your very soul.

Here are nine points of leverage to improve self-concept and increase self-esteem; some we have already discussed. They are:

Intrinsic motivation

Intrinsic motivation theory assumes that each individual is inherently motivated towards certain things and does not need an external push. Engaging in pursuits toward which you are inherently motivated (and that are not bad!) increases self-esteem. Change sweeps over and past you when you are doing what you really want to do.

Self-knowledge

Self-knowledge, including knowing your heritage, accepting your strengths, and acknowledging your vulnerabilities, increases your immunity to self-deception. You gain an accurate self-concept, and know where you stand.

Self talk

You can influence your confidence and actions and view of yourself (your self-esteem) by the things you say to yourself about yourself and about your future. You can use new labels and reminder systems to reinforce your new self image.

Locus of control

With high self-esteem, you put the center of control of your life inside yourself, not outside yourself. Even so, you can also be very trusting and willing to submit to a higher power or to others whom you respect. You feel a sense of control, and able to choose your path and attitude in the face of change.

Managing sources of self-esteem

You can choose your sources of self-esteem. You can lend little or no credence to some inputs, and you can pay close attention to others.

The Wisdom of K. Hieronymus

Remember IALAC—I Am Loveable And Capable. Remember it especially in the midst of hard change.

Self-esteem can be summarized as "I feel lovable, and I feel capable."

This approach comprises the worthiness component. The most powerful way of looking at self is with reference to a higher power, something outside yourself, something bigger than you are.

When you do things that are compatible with what you consider honest and moral behavior, you feel good about yourself. When you feel worthy, you feel better about yourself and your potential in all ways.

Significant others

Listen to those whose opinions you should value. In particular, give credence to those who are positive about your skills and attributes, and who care about you. Choose your significant others wisely.

If those around you do not make you feel better about yourself, or make you want to do better, find others.

Accomplishments/goals ratio

Each person grades differently. Some are "easy graders;" others are harsh in how they assess themselves to be, compared to how they think they should be.

If you constantly set your goals too high, out of reach, you will always fall short. Too low, and you will not feel that you have accomplished much. The ratio of intentions to completions is another way of expressing this. This relates to the degree to which you actually complete what you say you are going to complete. One part of this aspect of your self-esteem is your perceived potential, which is always your potential by when. The question is—how well are you doing now compared to how well you think you should be doing now? How hard should you be on yourself? Be accurate but kind in self-judgment.

Task intimacy

Task intimacy is the degree to which you totally embrace tasks (your work, paid or otherwise), for your own reasons and to your own standard of excellence. Respect whatever task you are engaged in.

Service

Giving service to others never fails to make you feel better about yourself, and more grateful for what you have.

LIFE TOOLS™
Use consistently until they become your tools for life

1. Schedule more time with people who make you feel good about yourself or make you feel desire and confidence to do better. Spend less time with people who make you feel inferior or bad. Feed opportunities; starve problems.

2. Keep a shoebox (or a file folder, or paper bag, or drawer) that contains positive notes from others, or records of accomplishments. Read through them periodically.

3. If you admire or are grateful for or appreciative of another's character or actions, express it. As an experiment, raise their self-esteem by sharing your positive perception. Do this for a week and notice how this makes you feel about yourself.

4. Remember the positive voices of your childhood. Remember those experiences when you drew positive conclusions about yourself. Write them down.

5. Develop your own personal language to confidently describe yourself. Finish the sentence—I am... with ten phrases. Put the list away, then do it twice more, at least two days apart. Look at all your lists at once. Put the five that you like best on an index card and post it where you can see it often.

6. Adjust your accomplishments to goals ratio-—do you have to accomplish at 100% efficiency to feel good about yourself, or is 51% OK? Set your goals lower or higher. Choose standards and evaluation methods that are within your control.

7. Become better grounded in your heritage. Learn the stories of your childhood. Learn the stories of your forebears. Be grateful for the contribution and sacrifice of those who have gone before. Seek out someone who can tell the stories, or find a written source. If some are not written down, write them down.

8. Choose to interpret your tasks in a way that makes you part of something bigger than yourself. Write a sentence about your perspective. Then do your best, allowing for those instances when competing priorities or health limits you.

9. Choose to serve and encourage others. Find ways to raise the esteem of others. Offer praise and give credit liberally. Create a rising tide and it will float all boats to a higher level.

TRAPS

Avoid the trap of over-achievement. If you find yourself feeling that you never do enough, or that what you do is never good enough, you might be falling victim to this trap. Step back, take a deep physical and emotional breath, and reevaluate. Be open to concluding that what you have already done is just fine.

Beware the trap of paralysis by analysis. Don't dwell on negative thoughts or inputs. Take action. Do something that makes another feel good about himself, or that makes you feel good about yourself.

Remember: persistent resistance to change brings atrophy and death. Using change as a way to learn more about yourself brings growth and life.

PERPETUAL ENCOURAGEMENT

In what you decide to think about, focus on the positive.

Know that you are unique. Be willing to consider the possibility that you have a mission to fulfill, a contribution to make, that is different from that of every other person on the planet.

Some will criticize you. Remember, the criticism is because of them and their view of the world, not you. Take it as input, not gospel. Or as interesting data about them!

"That which you persist in doing becomes easier, not that the task itself has become easier, but that our ability to perform it has improved." - Ralph Waldo Emerson

APPENDIX

"No one can make you feel inferior without your permission" - **Eleanor Roosevelt**

Self-perception is personally derived. What is derived dictates the quality of change resilience. Two people can have the same experience, and reach entirely different conclusions about themselves. Be aware of the malleability of self-perception and the positive or negative nature of your conclusions.

In seeing yourself as part of something bigger, remember the story about the three bricklayers. One was laying bricks, the next was making a wall, and the third was building a cathedral. They were working side by side.

SUMMARY

1. Self-concept is a personal, hopeful, and balanced view of self that leads you to accept who you are and to feel positive about your potential.

2. Self-esteem is personally derived, drawn from a realistic self concept and from action that helps you discover and express who you are.

3. Self-esteem is preserved by conclusions about yourself..

4. The levers of self-esteem are intrinsic motivation, self knowledge, self talk, locus of control, managing sources of self-esteem, significant others, accomplishments/goals ratio, task intimacy and service.

5. Of all of the above, the quickest, surest path to self-esteem is giving service to others.

PRINCIPLE 8:

Drive Closure

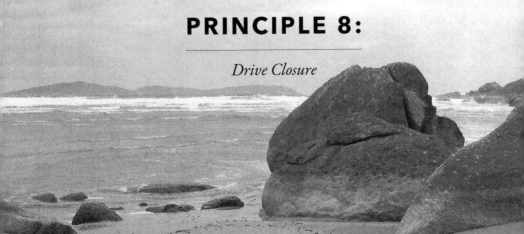

Tie up loose ends. Finish what is unfinished...or let it go. Bring open items
to closure. Resolve breaches. Resolve conflicts. Forgive others. Do not let hurt
linger. Let go and move on. Repent. Keep up to date. Doing these things
magnifies your resilience in the face of change and brings lasting peace.

SONGLINE
Learn to navigate the wilderness of change

The story is told of two monks who were taking a day's journey to a distant town to conduct business for the monastery. When they had joined the monastery, they had each taken a vow of poverty, charity, and chastity. Part of their commitment included not touching a woman in any manner, except to shake hands. They had been monks for some time and were well committed to their vows.

On their journey, towards afternoon, they came to a wide and swift river, which was waist deep and treacherous with slippery stones. At the edge of the river they found a beautiful young woman weeping and staring out across the water.

Upon inquiring, they learned that she needed to cross the river to visit her sick mother, who lived in a village on the other shore. She begged them to carry her across. The first monk refused, because of his vows. The second monk listened to her plea, then straightaway reached out his arms, picked her up, told her to clasp her arms around his neck, and carried her across. He set her down, acknowledged her thanks, took his leave and moved on.

The first monk could not believe what had just happened. As they continued their journey, he chastised his brother, reminding him of his vows, criticizing him for holding the woman. He went on and on.

Finally the second monk stopped, clasped his fellow monk on the shoulder, looked him full in the face, and said, "Yes, I touched a woman in a way that was contrary to my vows. I held her for some time. But when I got to the other side of the river, I put her down and moved on, and you are still carrying her!"

Moving on is an important change skill. Change often uncovers the need to move on by revealing the obsolescence of your current set of beliefs and practices. The situation changes, there are new sets of demands, and what you are doing no longer works. Time to move on.

To respond to the demands of change, you will often need to change your approach. Change might reveal a personal weakness. You might need to switch priorities. Available resources change; you have more to do than time allows. You might need to "carry things" that you normally would not. You need to put down one thing, and shift your energy to another thing.

Or you might make mistakes. Usually daily. Progress and happiness consist of accepting, acknowledging, learning, correcting, letting go, and moving on.

Or you might be tempted to linger. You might hang on too long to what is actually finished, hoping for a different reality. Instead, you need to move on. Let go and allow closure.

Bringing closure is a skill that frees up energy for new pursuits. It prepares us for the unexpected changes of life. It gives us power in the face of life's unreliability.

Once my grandfather talked about some farm work he had done for a relative, involving a team of horses, for which he had never been compensated. I think the amount was $20 in 1930's money. Something

The Wisdom of K. Hieronymus

You may have repented and thoroughly changed, and forgiven self, and still not have "memory closure." That is OK. Having the memory helps you to persist in progress. So long as you do not let the memory take negative hold on your self-esteem.

Or, you may have forgiven another, but still remember the hurt. Use it as wisdom, as a warning of what to avoid in the future, or as a way to recognize what situations to be alert to as change evolves.

happened that he had not been paid immediately, then the obligation drifted and was never fulfilled. It had been decades. It was still an open issue. It still bothered him. I am not sure the matter ever came to closure. I think he took it to his grave. Perhaps the matter has since been resolved in a face to face conversation.

Loss often accompanies change. You lose friends, possessions, privileges. You lose opportunities.

You can mourn the loss for years or decades, or do something different. You can immediately accept the loss, take stock of the current situation, resolve it in your mind, create closure, then move on.

Someone in your past might have offended you. They might have "trespassed against you." There are those who are unfeeling, unskilled, ill-intentioned, insensitive or even evil in their intention. They have wronged us. And they might never change. The time has come to declare closure and move on.

Hurts that linger tend to fester. Energy caught up in the past is not present and not available for current change challenges.

When you set new goals or tackle a new project, you often do not fulfill your intention. Sometimes the goal was too high; sometimes other priorities intervened, sometimes you should wisely abandon the goal. Regret over non-achievement, or over lost opportunities, can linger for a long time, sapping your energy and diverting your focus from the important matters of today. Instead, move on.

APPLICATION
Employ this principle to benefit you and those you love

When is finished really finished? Being finished is a process.

The process of closure has three steps. They are:

1. Recognize and accept that you need to resolve—bring closure to— something. In some cases this can require asking for counsel from someone who is wiser than you or who has more life experience in the matter you are struggling with. Sometimes just the act of admitting your shortfall verbally to another, getting it on the table and out into the open, jump-starts the closure process. This person can also help you think through the lengths you must go to in completing the next two steps. In other cases this means simply making a list of things that are unfinished.

    This can be a list of tasks to be finished, new things to take on, decisions to be made, feelings to be resolved, relationships to end or strengthen, clutter to be cleared, practices to abandon or continue, or messages to deliver.

2. In the case of things you have done or are doing that you need to change, or that need to be resolved, change course. If you have trespassed against another, make amends as best you can. Put new things on your calendar. Restore what was lost or destroyed to the best of your ability. This includes speaking to those you have trespassed against, if they are still alive and available to you. It may also include asking forgiveness. Whether or not the person grants forgiveness makes no difference. You have done your part. In the case of your list of unfinished items, go directly at the thing. Set priorities and decide what to do. Take action. Hold necessary conversations. Don't try to do everything all at once—set priorities, pick your battles, decide what will have to wait. But do what you can. Do all you can

given the circumstances. Then walk away or let it alone. Await the result in peace.

3.   Do all you can to sustain the new attitude/behavior from that time forward. This is a lifelong quest—as you begin, your energy will build, and it becomes an exciting and fulfilling lifelong quest. Replace old behavior with new behavior, don't just remove the old behavior. Nature abhors a vacuum. Old ways will rush back in if you do not redirect the energy. If you slip, and fall back into old ways, repeat the steps. Eventually, the new ways will stick.

Take personal responsibility for initiating and completing the closure process. Do not expect others to make the change. I once was part of an organization where one of the corporate norms was "clean up your own messes." That meant you were expected to resolve any rift of your own making that inhibited a productive working relationship with a colleague or client. The test of whether anything was outstanding was whether we would seek or avoid contact with that person.

When I had my therapy practice, a woman once came to me to discuss severe family relationship problems with her spouse and daughter. I quickly became aware that she had unresolved hurt from her relationship with her father. It was clear that she needed to take the initiative to heal the breach. She resisted, and disclosed that she had not talked with him for more than 10 years, and did not even know where he lived. I strongly urged her to consider trying to locate him and initiate contact. She said she would think about it.

The next day I received a phone call from this woman. She was in tears. Her father had just called her and asked if he could come visit. They had set a date. The breach began to heal a few weeks later with his visit.

Coming to closure with parents is an important life task that brings a sense of completeness and peace. Most children have unresolved issues with their parents well into their 30's. Take the plunge and talk it out. Do not be discouraged if they do not immediately understand your distress. Be patient, respectful, and compassionate about how hard it is to be a good parent.

Forgiving others is a prime part of moving on. Forgiving others is part of the resolution process. Not forgiving others, declining to just let it go, hurts us, not them.

I was once part of a household moving company in New York City. My two "partners" were Hispanic friends. We often made comments on the items we were moving, in a language that none of our customers could understand.

When we came across something that was obviously junk, that we could not believe we were being paid to move, our inside joke was—"Este es una cosa de mucho valor sentimental!" (This is an item of much sentimental value). I am not sure the joke translates, but the concept translates—be judicious in holding onto things whose value might have expired.

Hanging on to things, to "stuff," is an affliction of our times. For a long time there has been a documented surplus of clothing in the world. There is a surplus of clothing in most of our closets. Not to mention other stuff in our houses, attics, car trunks, and garages—knick-knacks, bowls, flowers, pictures, extra tools, figurines, just-in-case items.

Learn to let things go, turn them loose, "release them to the universe" so others can use them. Take them to a thrift store or hold a yard sale. Putting something back into circulation takes away clutter, distraction, and drag, like scraping barnacles off of the bottom of a boat, so that the boat cuts more cleanly through the water.

LIFE TOOLS™
Use consistently until they become your tools for life

1. This is actually a 2-part task that takes some time, but it is one of the most energizing and liberating tasks you can carry out. Make a list of open items, things that are not finished. You can start by purchasing or otherwise obtaining a notebook of some sort.

   Title the first page—"OPEN ITEMS." Then list a category on each succeeding page—such as house, car, medical, dental, spouse, ex.-spouse, parents, work, recreation, etc. Be totally and utterly comprehensive. Then send me an email at lorinrwalker@gmail.com for further instructions.

2. Pick one unresolved thing in your life and follow the three-step process listed in the application section above. Be courageous (proceeding forward despite fear). Seek help from a higher power. You will be amazed at the positive impact, relief and peace that eventually comes.

3.   Pretend that you have 10 life "do-overs" (like a Mulligan in golf). In other words, looking back at your life, you can do 10 things differently.

Make a two column list. In the 1st column, list the 10 things.

In the 2nd column, list what you would do differently. Then, look at the 2nd column and ask yourself if you are now the kind of person, with requisite motivation, knowledge and wisdom, that you would actually now do that thing differently. If yes, take comfort. If no, decide what you need to change so that you would be that kind of person. Taking action in this regard leads to a feeling of completeness, wholeness and preparation.

4.   Clean and sort through your closets, clean your drawers, thoroughly clean your car, or sort through your garage or attic. Release unnecessary or obsolete things to the universe through a yard sale or just give them away.

5.   Take advantage of quiet moments (or create them on your schedule!). In a quiet moment, ask yourself what you can do better or differently, a relationship you can heal, a hurt you can ease, a personal improvement, etc. Often this involves being meek and lowly of heart, admitting mistakes, showing kindness and simply letting your better impulses assert themselves. Follow through on your impressions.

6.   Make a list, entitled "What is Finished"? Be comprehensive. Let this be a liberating experience. Free yourself from the tendrils of the past. Write all of these things on a piece (or pieces) of paper. Go into the back yard, or to a park, and set fire to the paper. Scatter the ashes.

TRAPS

Surprisingly, one of the most prevalent traps is to overdo the closure process: to make your list of things to change too long, to be too hard on yourself, to be too critical, too perfectionistic. Guard against this.

Do not let anger linger. In the words of **William Blake**:

"I was angry with my friend.

I told my friend, my wrath did end.

I was angry with my foe.

I told it not, my wrath did grow."

Beware of being resistant to closure. Persistent resistance to closure keeps you stuck in the past, and eventually brings atrophy and death. Using change as a way to learn more about what you can do differently or better, and embracing its energy for the welfare of self and others, brings growth and life.

PERPETUAL ENCOURAGEMENT

In what you decide to think about, focus on the positive.

Know that you are unique. Be willing to consider the possibility that you have a mission to fulfill, a contribution to make, that is different from that of every other person on the planet.

Sometimes just making a decision, any decision, even if it isn't exactly what you wanted, is a relief. It brings closure.

"That which you persist in doing becomes easier, not that the task itself has become easier, but that our ability to perform it has improved." - **Ralph Waldo Emerson**

APPENDIX

"Holding a grudge makes you a drudge". - Unknown

Sign posted in the window of a custom furniture shop. "Finishers Wanted"

"Remember O Lord, thy tender mercies...remember not the sins of my youth." - 25th Psalm, King James Bible

"Half of the unhappiness in life comes from people being afraid to go straight at things." - **William J. Lock**

SUMMARY

1. Take stock of unfinished things in your life. This may be for the whole of your life or for those things on your immediate plate. These may be wrong actions or mistakes you have been aware of for some time; or things you are recently aware of. At the same time, take care to not be too perfectionistic nor hard on yourself.

2. Another way to do step one is to notice the kinds of change in your life that are hardest for you to handle. Ask yourself what aspects of your character or approach, if changed, would make you more resilient.

3. Seek help from a higher power.

4. Decide which of these things needs immediate action, or which things you are most motivated and able to take action on.

5. Bring closure. This usually means talking to someone, or changing behavior and replacing it with new behavior. In some cases, it means simply declaring or allowing closure. In other cases, it might mean standing up for yourself, declaring victory, and discerning or accepting that you need do nothing different.

6. Establish a support system. This could meaning sharing your change desire with a trusted person, or it could mean creating a reminder system (described in chapter one) to cement the change in place. It also means replacing old things or behavior with new things or behavior.

7. Be ready for resistance as you change, from yourself and others. Do not let the opposition of resistance stop you.

8. Be in the mode of constantly learning and repenting.

9. Taking action and bringing closure creates a feeling of completeness, closure, wholeness, and peace. But sometimes, at the beginning, fear. Keep moving forward. Rejoice in and relish this feeling.

PRINCIPLE 9:

Learn Constantly

Constantly search out new learnings. Appreciate the world as a giant heuristic (self-teaching) device, loaded with learning opportunities. Let change be your stimulus and partner in learning. Choose to live in a world of facts. Deal with what is really there. Everyone knows how to do something you do not. Watch them and take notes. Decide that every change, no matter what, is a learning opportunity. Be always hungry, on the lookout, for wisdom. Be open to learning and it will find you.

SONGLINE

Learn to navigate the wilderness of change

When my father was in high school, he ran out of things to read. He looked in the library, and discovered a set of books with the word "encyclopedia" in the title. He read them all.

This was not a one-time fluke. He was constantly motivated to learn to do what was before him to do. He made change and challenge his friends as he grew in capacity. Things that others had gone to four years of college to learn, he learned on the job, acquiring the equivalent in knowledge of a bachelor's degree in electrical engineering.

To grow in happiness, peace, and power, you must be willing to learn new things; there is no other way. To grow in change resilience, you must be willing not only to learn new things, but also to apply the things you learn. The net effect will be more power to appreciate life and contribute to others' lives.

The opposite, to resist learning, causes atrophy. To atrophy means to waste away or to be arrested in development.

The story is told of a young scholar who was able to secure an audience with a great and gifted teacher. In his first meeting, he asked the learned man what he needed to do to gain great knowledge and wisdom. The teacher said not a word, but motioned to the young man to follow him. They walked together out into the ocean until they were waist deep. The teacher, though old, was wiry and strong. Without warning, he grasped the young man and plunged him under the water and held him there. The pupil struggled and fought for breath. He flailed wildly and bubbles of air escaped through his mouth and nostrils. Finally, when his strength was spent, he found himself lifted above the surface, and took in great gulps of air.

When he had recovered the capacity to speak, sputtering and gasping, he angrily demanded why the scholar had done that. With a kindly look in his eye, the learned man replied, "When you are as hungry for knowledge as you were for air, you will acquire great knowledge and wisdom."

So it is with us. We must be hungry for great gulps of knowledge. When we desire knowledge and wisdom as much as we desire oxygen, we will gain the knowledge and wisdom needed for growth, peace, and happiness.

We must put aside our hunger for - easily digested, pre-packaged knowledge-bits, or learning only from structured classroom situations as the only way to learn. Much of our food these days comes prepackaged; at times we like our knowledge the same way—in sound bytes of 20 seconds or less, or in classroom sessions of 50 minutes or less. But food for the body and food for the mind are different things. We must discard the notion that knowledge must be a pre-packaged commodity. We must embrace all sources, no matter how unlikely.

Change often reveals the obsolescence of our current set of beliefs and practices. It creates lack of air, as it were. Demands on us change, what we are doing is no longer working—new knowledge, new perspective is crucial. Learning allows us to understand, endure, and then move on, which are important change skills. Motivation to pursue new knowledge is one of change's greatest gifts.

Sometimes the "truth of truth" is not immediately evident. We must also be willing to struggle with the truth, like Jacob in his wrestle with the angel of God, before truth is ours. Sometimes we must persistently ask a question, for days, months, or even years, before the illumination enlightens.

We often lazily and gullibly accept that just because another is able to throw a ball with great speed and accuracy, or can convincingly impersonate someone else (as an actor), or has great good looks or is good at telling jokes, that this person is also wise in the ways of deodorant, razor blades, child rearing, fashion, or politics.

There is a "phenom" in back country navigating known as "bending the map." A hiker becomes lost, and then, in panic and a desire to be not-lost and in control, fits the map to the surrounding terrain, instead of admitting they are lost, evaluating the terrain according to the facts of the map, and finding the way out. This twisting of the truth to fit personal prejudice or desire has proven fatal at times. Learn and conform to the facts, accept things as they really are. Admit when you are lost.

Be persistent. I have a friend who is the mother of seven children, who embraces that responsibility, works long hours every week, and is also in a full-time college nursing program. She constantly displays grit in her quest for knowledge. She is right at the top of her class, a rigorous program from which almost half have dropped out. She has been rocked with change over the last two years—family challenges, health challenges, and financial challenges. She soldiers on. Her commitment to learning and growth are phenomenal and inspiring.

APPLICATION
Employ this principle to bene-fit you and those you love

To learn is one of life's two great imperatives and greatest joys. The other is to form positive and lasting relationships. Both are interrelated. Doing one creates power and opportunity for the other.

Seek all kinds of learning: not just in the library or laboratory or only from books, not only from discourse or lecture, but all learning—-by experience, by precept, by correction, from watching others' example—all of the above, in balance.

The Wisdom of K. Hieronymus

Everything you learn prepares you to learn more. Knowledge in one field will always cross over and deepen your knowledge—or perspective–in all fields. No learning is wasted; it will connect to and enrich other learning. Be open to experience and learning in fields that are completely outside your current experience or preference. No effort at learning is ever wasted; at the least, you will learn how to learn...or how not to learn.

If you hold the world to be a place that constantly shifts to grant you learning opportunities, you cannot lose. No matter what change may bring, you can and will learn from everything that happens. You will welcome every change, no matter how "unwelcome," and use it as a learning opportunity.

The process of learning has five protocols. They are:

1. **Cultivate a "Holy Curiosity":**

    Look for the things that are good and true. Pursue what is lovely and virtuous. There are many "ugly truths." Acknowledge them as facts; do not fill your mind with them. Give place for truths that edify, enlighten or point to possibilities. Through it all, accept change as your partner in learning.

2. **Know what you want to know—scope out what you need or want to learn:**

    Create a learning plan or structure. Sometimes signing up for a class or a program of instruction automatically gives you a plan or structure. Or reading a series of books can do that (like my father's encyclopedias). Or create your own plan and structure. This does not always have to be written down; it could be invented "on the fly." You might discover as you go.

3. **Seek opportunities to learn daily, and make yourself open to all positive sources:**

    Find a teacher (do not trust all teachers—do your homework, follow your intuition), sign up for a course of study. Start reading and listening and learning. Subscribe to a magazine. Join a book club.

    Learning is a lifelong quest, and not always easy—as you explore new knowledge, your energy builds to learn even more, and it becomes an exciting and fulfilling lifelong quest. But you must put in the time.

4. **Apply and share what you have learned:**

    Live what you have learned. Place yourself in conformity to the new knowledge. Share with and serve others with the knowledge. Teach it.

5. **Finally (or maybe firstly), accept change as your partner-in-learning:**

    Whenever a change happens, especially a Type IV (unexpected, unwelcome) change, ask yourself, "What is the learning opportunity in this experience?"

In all your learning, learn to discern. Do not take things at face value. Ask questions about others' motives. If you are OK with the motives, ask yourself what their underlying assumptions might be. Test those assumptions against things you know to be true.

Choose to live in a world of facts. Deal with what is really there. Do not bend the map. Do not deny what is really so (denial is not just a river in Egypt!). There is a lot of wrong opinion and false perception out there. Many people work hard to shade and hide the truth. The truth, what really is, is precious and powerful. Do not accept less.

Confront truth. Get things out on the table. Note: to confront means to bring something to the front, to fully examine it, to allow it to unconceal itself in all its being. Confrontation need not be contentious. Do not ignore the truth.

Many facts in the world are to be found in books. Unfortunately, many books that claim to do not contain facts, but conjecture, supposition, or outright lies. This applies even more to the internet, where the barrier to entry is so much lower.

Learn to learn. When I first arrived in New York City, to start a challenging course of study at an Ivy League University, I became aware of how much more I should have paid attention in class in high school, and how much harder I should have worked outside of class. It was a sometimes wrenching adjustment.

Fortunately, there were those from my home state who had arrived before me and encountered similar challenges. They taught me how to survive in an immensely challenging intellectual environment. I was issued an IDAHO POWER button (literally) and a set of mimeographed learning instructions. These were things such as "do not sit and read for more than three hours at a time—after that, get up, take a break, take a short walk, clear your head, then resume. In class, listening to a lecture, mentally question and argue with the teacher. Jot down your counter-arguments for later perusal. Look for contrast, comparisons, similarities in ideas, gaps. Remember, you are learning how to think!"

Later, I was coached on how to read a book—"Do not think you need to read a book cover to cover, sequentially from first page to last. As you begin, ask yourself why you are reading this book—what is the purpose and the hoped-for knowledge? Then read the table of contents. Which parts are most pertinent to your purpose? Are there summary chapters that can be the foundation for your understanding?

Then read the book in priority order. Skim examples once you have the gist. Make notes in the margin and underline key points. Write notes to yourself. Etc."

Later, I learned the wisdom sequence—as we persist in wanting to know, data becomes information becomes knowledge becomes wisdom.

LIFE TOOLS™
Use consistently until they become your tools for life

1. If you have previously discontinued a course of learning, resume and finish it.

2. Schedule yourself to listen to something that is completely opposite your normal interests or beliefs. For example, listen to a lecture or watch a program that espouses views you oppose. Seek to understand the logic and point of view.

3. Volunteer to teach a class or lead a discussion.

4.	Schedule yourself for two hours in the nearest public library, perhaps on a regular basis. Go to the magazine section. Browse. Take notes if desired.

5.	Seek out a teacher who knows more than you in a field of interest. Ask questions.

6.	Set aside a quiet time every morning, or whenever you feel most alert. Meditate. Read some text that is inspiring or sacred to you. Pray for direction.

7.	Make a list of ten books you have always wanted to read. Write the numbers 1-10 next to the titles, in priority order. Notice what happens.

8.	Subscribe to a book club or join a discussion group.

9.	Sign up for a class, a degree program or other course of study, or volunteer to learn something in your employment that will be useful to your co-workers or clients. Become expert in something new.

10.	Purchase a series of tapes or CDs or DVDs that are of interest to you. Or check them out of the library. Listen in your car. Watch them on your computer.

11.	Set a time each day to watch the news or the history or geography channel, or establish a web routine, visiting a series of websites each day.

TRAPS

Do not fall into the ancient traps that many have warned against—"After their own lusts shall they heap to themselves teachers, having itching ears...led away with divers lusts, ever learning, and never able to come to the knowledge of the truth...and shall be turned unto fables." - King James Bible, 2 Timothy 3: 6-7, 4: 3-4

Beware of false teachers and easy knowledge. Beware of the sound byte, the quick quip, the clever retort of the celebrity or the glib explanation of the politician.

PERPETUAL ENCOURAGEMENT

See the world to be a place that constantly moves to grant you learning opportunities. Thus, you cannot lose: no matter what happens, you can, you will, learn from it. Welcome these opportunities.

Learn from your successes as well as failures. Reframe failure as "Nothing more than an opportunity to begin again, with new knowledge." - Henry Ford.

Move forward. Resist resistance. Doubt doubt. Deny denial.

Fear, doubt, and discomfort can be the beginning of wisdom.

Seeking counsel often is a sign of strength, not weakness.

APPENDIX

"Reading maketh a full man; conference a ready man; and writing an exact man." - Francis Bacon

"Man's mind, stretched by a new idea, never goes back to its original dimensions." - Oliver Wendell Holmes, Jr.

"Truth is knowledge of things as they are, as they were, and as they are to come." - Joseph Smith, Jr.

"In all thy getting get understanding." - Proverbs 4:7

"We learn "precept upon precept, line upon line, here a little there a little". - Isaiah 28:13

"[Wisdom] crieth at the gates...receive my instruction, and not silver; and knowledge rather than choice gold." - Proverbs 8:1,3,10

SUMMARY

1. Learning is one of life's two great imperatives. The other is forming positive and lasting relationships.

2. Desire learning as much as you desire oxygen.

3. Use every occasion, especially those created by change, as learning opportunities. Always be on the lookout for new learning.

4. Do not be afraid of the truth, even if it is frightening or uncomfortable. The truth will set you free, but it may make you quite angry first. Accept what is true; adjust and move forward.

5. Learning a new attitude is at least as important as learning new knowledge.

6. Follow the five "learning protocols":

    - Cultivate a holy curiosity.
    - Scope out what you want to learn.
    - Seek opportunities to learn daily and always.
    - Apply and share what you have learned, using the knowledge to serve and others.
    - Accept change as your partner-in-learning.

7. Learn to learn and look beneath the surface. Discount celebrity.

8. Learn something new every day, all your life. at the end of every day, ask yourself, "What new thing did I learn today"?

9. Use your learning to help you serve others.

PRINCIPLE 10:

Design Fulfillment Structures

Make plans and set goals. Expect and incorporate change and the unexpect-ed as a matter of course. Focus on priorities, based on G-stress goals. Do first things first. Prepare every needful thing. Keep track. Monitor a completions list. Be organized and help others be the same. Being organized and keeping up to date enhances your resilience in the face of change.

SONGLINE
Learn to navigate the wilderness of change

"To the summit and safe return. To the summit and safe return. To the summit and safe return."

That is the mantra that Lene Gammelgaard established and said often to herself months previous to her 1996 attempt on the summit of Mount Everest. And she kept saying it as the trek progressed. She kept saying it as she barely survived one of the most deadly days in the history of Everest, when eight climbers died. She made it to the summit and returned safely.

More than 250 people are known to have died on Everest. Many die on the way down. Some are just unlucky, but many had failed to create a fulfillment structure to take them to completion. Many had not thought beyond the summit. Lene had.

Lene had the mantra; she also created a fulfillment structure that fulfilled the mantra—all the way to the end.

She started creating the structure years earlier, laying the mental, physical, emotional, and financial foundation—and the affiliative foundation, i.e. how she chose her companions. Ultimately, it was her fellow climbers who sustained her will to fulfill.

Effective fulfillment structures take us all the way to the end. And beyond.

As the saying goes—failing to plan is planning to fail. This is not always true, of course; sometimes we get lucky. But luck tends to favor the prepared and planful.

Most of us will never do anything as dramatic as reaching the summit of Everest. Unless you count gaining an education, raising children, taking care of parents and siblings, developing your character, magnifying your talents, surviving setbacks, learning from everything that happens to you, serving others, positively affecting other lives, and surviving and thriving through tens of thousands of unexpected change events!! You get the picture.

What are our mantras and what is the structure that will carry us gallantly through all of these changes and challenges?

It has been said that Arnold Schwarzenegger is not an actor; he is a presence. He developed that presence through accomplishment. He created the accomplishments with a priority fulfillment structure based upon index cards.

At the beginning of his career, he wrote down what he wanted to accomplish—this included things such as "learn better English (English better?), win the Mr. Universe contest, win a significant political office, marry a remarkable woman, etc. Every day, he would take out those cards and read them, and use that day to further that vision. This was a large measure of his fulfillment structure. Fulfillment structures do not need to be elaborate. They just need to be followed.

Everyone reading this book follows some sort of priority fulfillment structure, or you would not be reading this book.

Some would do well to simply follow better the structure they have in place; others would do well to revamp their structure; others are in serious trouble and need a serious structure makeover.

Many have been rocked by change, and the shock waves continue, even as new change takes aim, including the unexpected that will transpire later today or tomorrow.

New structures are needed.

The Wisdom of K. Hieronymus

Leave a few open spaces each day for the unexpected. Things will change. Meetings or obligations will arise and need attention. Also be prepared to take advantage of "positive-additive time" as meetings or obligations disappear, leaving you with a "gift of time." If there is nothing important and urgent to attend to, relax and meditate upon your blessings and goals.

In carrying out your day, in addition to doing first things first, do worst things first— then you will stop dreading them, and the rest of the day will be the easiest part of the day. Said another way, always eat a live toad first thing in the morning. Then nothing worse will happen to you all day.

Know when it is time to rest, and take a breather; when leaving a task, leave it in such a state that you can quickly and easily pick it back up.

Remember— Busyness is not a virtue. Being busy with priorities is a virtue.

There are many who have tackled this subject. You can find numerous books, numerous systems of priority fulfillment, often called things like time management. All of them have things to offer. Most are built on a simple 3-part formula—make a list, prioritize, start on the first item.

When we set new goals, or tackle a new project, we often do not fulfill our intention. Sometimes the goal was too high; sometimes other priorities intervene, sometimes we wisely abandon the goal. Regret over non-achievement, or over lost opportunities, can linger for a long time, sapping our energy and diverting our focus from the important matters of today. It is important to move on.

APPLICATION
Employ this principle to benefit you and those you love

My first wife had a great fulfillment structure. Several, in fact, suited to the task and to the energy she had available. They were multi-tiered and fit-for-purpose. She accomplished an enormous amount.

For example, when it was a day of many tasks that were not necessarily connected, she used the yellow highlight method:

She typed a list of everything that needed doing that day or soon. She chose a font size large enough that it can be seen from a distance of six feet so she could glance at it. When an item was completed, she highlighted it in bright yellow.

From a distance, at a glance, she could see what was done, and what remained. The yellow-highlighted items served as both a record and a motivation.

When it was a day for reflection, thinking forward, anticipating planned events and also the unexpected (change), she used a traditional calendared book method, with one page for each day of the year and an accompanying monthly calendar. She laid the foundation for accomplishment. She combined trips and related tasks. She was not a time-nut automaton, far from it. She had all the interruptible time in the world for her brood of seven-plus and for friends and for students of her artistry.

She had also learned the value of looking forward to things. This was often something months in advance—"To the seminar and safe return. To the seminar and safe return. To the summit (er, seminar) and safe return."

And most importantly, she kept moving.

She had learned to harness the power of a priority fulfillment structure.

Fulfillment structures consist of three parts. The parts are: plan, do, flex:

1. **Plan:** Schedule quiet time. Schedule time to "waste." Plan in moments of serenity. Execute in moments of energy. Think of life in terms of projects.

2. **Do:** In the case of your list of unfinished items, go directly at the thing. Set priorities and decide what to do. Take action. Hold necessary conversations. Don't try to do everything, and don't try to do things all at once—set priorities, pick your battles, decide what will have to wait. But do what you can. Do all you can, given the circumstances. Then walk away or let it alone. Await the result in peace.

3. **Flex:** Priorities change, resources change, you have more to do than time allows. You often must put down one thing, and shift your energy to another thing.

It has been said that no plan survives contact with the enemy. In this case, the "enemy" is the chaotic and rich mix of the unexpected and unplanned-for change and opportunity that we call life—the things that happen every day that bring newness, novelty and the unexpected into our existence. New opportunities will arise, new challenges will call for your effort. Change will have its way. You must adjust your goals, your actions, and your timing. This is all to the good.

Further thoughts on planning, doing, and flexing:

> A noted author in the field of human behavior described his method as follows: "I always schedule a couple of days to "waste" at the beginning of a writing project. This is my time to think things through, to jot down notes, to scribble, to play with ideas, many of which will later be discarded in the process of the writing itself. This is the foundation time. Once I have wasted that time, I get started (I have already started)."

> Another accomplished writer, this time in the field of music, described his method of doing: "I schedule certain blocks of time for certain activities. I may have one hour for one piece; another hour or two to create another portion. I may block out time for correspondence with a publisher. Whatever the time allotted, no matter where I am when the "timer" goes off, I stop. I save the remainder of the task for another day."

> Another person, an effective leader in a complex environment, uses the "book-list method" to organize both her planning and her doing. She carries a blank notebook with her everywhere. In the book, she jots down lists

of things to do, notes from meetings, impressions of things that need attention. She writes the date at the beginning of each entry. She has a code for the things that are her personal responsibility, another code for things to delegate to others. She reviews the book often, and brings to-do items as necessary into the current day.

Whatever your method, it is important to have a method. And it is important to follow it. Until you change it out for something superior.

Finally, recognize that most things are either urgent, important, or both. What seems important is often just masquerading as urgent. It may not really be an important, immediate priority. What is important (such as car maintenance, marriage maintenance, career maintenance, or child maintenance!) may not seem urgent, but it is. Spend your time on the important. Be suspicious of the urgent.

LIFE TOOLS™
Use consistently until they become your tools for life

1. Plan during moments of clarity, refine during moments of spirituality (strokes of insight), execute during moments of opportunity and energy.

    What is your best time of insight during a "normal" day? schedule that time on your calendar, and use it to plan and to be inspired—e.g., to make lists, prioritize, ponder on priorities. Revisit and refine as necessary as you execute your plan during the day.

2. Make a life-list, which is a list of 12-20 things that you want to accomplish or experience by the end of your life. Post this list somewhere you will see it often. Update the list periodically. You can see my list at the end of this chapter.

3. Write a paragraph on three of your top lifetime goals or pursuits—include what, when, how. Put it in a drawer. Without looking at it, do the same thing again two days later. Put it away and wait two days. Then do it again, and when finished take out the other two and compare. Look for common themes. Create a final draft by cutting, pasting, and polishing. Then ask yourself—does my goal fulfillment structure support these goals/pursuits? Flex as needed.

4. Obtain a large, flat, monthly desktop calendar from an office supply store. Write down important dates and goals on the calendar for the next 3 months.

5. We are blessed in our time to have many priority fulfillment products commercially available. Explore them and pick one to use. Or go on a "research expedition"—pick and choose methods of fulfillment from the products available. Incorporate the ideas you like best. Then use some sort of system consistently.

6. At the beginning of every day, make a list, prioritize it; cross off items you complete.

7. Create a mantra, like Lene Gammelgaard did, in an area important to you.

8. Obtain a notebook and start the booklist method (described above).

9. The week is the microcosm of your life. Plan to do something each week that furthers your most important goals and fulfills parts of your most important roles. Plan these actions at the beginning of each week. Try it for three weeks. Note what happens.

TRAPS

Avoid the trap of "over-scheduling," of feeling that you must pack every second with activity. Notice the rhythm of the harvest. There is seed time, growth time, harvest time, and time for fields to lie fallow, at rest.

Fallow time is not unproductive time, it is a time of refurbishment and replenishment.

Beware the trap of excessive self-criticism if you don't get everything done.

You will never get everything done that is on your list—one of the wonderful things about the human mind is its capacity to conceive of more than it can achieve.

PERPETUAL ENCOURAGEMENT

Days are like suitcases: some people are able to pack more into them than others. A productive day can be "produced." We are all blessed with the capacity to think, imagine, conceive, plan, do, and adjust. The method does not matter; what matters is to have a method.

Try new things. You can always shift if it does not work. You will learn from anything new that you attempt.

APPENDIX

Example of a Life-List:

14 THINGS BEFORE I DIE

> *Kayak open water*
>
> *Backpack Alaska (done), Australia (done), Patagonia (December 2017)*
>
> *Attend the Final Four Championship*
>
> *Attend a digital photography workshop*
>
> *Design a piece of outdoor clothing (begun – fleece vest, bandana)*
>
> *Live with 3 Bonsai trees*
>
> *Paint 6 paintings I wouldn't mind displaying (begun – 4)*
>
> *Climb a Colorado Fourteener*
>
> *Write a book (begun)*
>
> *Own a titanium or carbon fiber bike (done)_*
>
> *Design & lead a personal/leadership growth workshop (done)*
>
> *Publish a book of poetry/dialogue/photos (begun)*
>
> *Sell a photo*
>
> *Sell a song*

SUMMARY

1.   Start to use a priority fulfillment structure. Or tinker with and improve the one you have.

2.   For the things that are important to you—At the beginning of each day, make a list, prioritize it, and cross off completions. Organize, prioritize, and accomplish in a logical fashion.

3.   For really important things, make use of a mantra, like "To the summit and safe return" to keep focus.

4.   Keep a calendar.

5.   Keep track of what is yet to complete.

6.   Plan in moments of clarity, do in moments of energy and opportunity, and always be ready to flex.

7.   Make a Life-List: 10 to 20 things you want to do or experience before you die. This will help you keep your priorities straight. This is not a wish list; it is a vision list.

8.   Do not spend time on things that are not priorities, but also know that sometimes priorities emerge from things that may at first seem unimportant. Follow your intuition when in doubt.

9.   Remember, busyness is not a virtue; being busy with priorities is a virtue.

PRINCIPLE 11:

Cultivate Humor

Humor eliminates or alleviates the pain and stress of change. Look for humor in all situations, especially the tough ones. When change throws challenges your way, find the laughter in the situation. Smile often. Bring a cheerful outlook to all challenges. Doing these things magnifies your resilience in the face of change and challenge and brings peace and joy.

SONGLINE
Learn to navigate the wilderness of change

Two cannibals were eating a clown. One turned to the other and said, "Does this taste funny to you?"

I still remember with fondness the person who told me this joke. It has been 14 years.

Humor lightens every load. Humor reduces the sting of tragedy. Humor binds audiences and groups and families together.

Humor creates resilience in the face of change. Humor reminds us that there is more than one way of looking at the world, and can materialize unexpectedly when the alternate worldview becomes apparent. Often the surprise worldview of humor is innocent and refreshing. On one occasion, when our five youngest children were small, we were sitting around the dinner table, and each child was telling those assembled about their day. We heard of exploits on the playground, the soccer field, in the classroom. One of the youngest boys was visibly about to burst with the desire to share something of note. Finally he blurted out, "And I don't have on any underwear!" And he didn't!

My father once endured a short stay in the hospital. Although in great pain with a serious illness, which eventually took his life, he did what he had done all his life—he found occasion for humor and sought opportunity to bring a little laughter to others. Towards the end of one particularly rough night, a nurse said to him, "You are driving me crazy!" His reply was, "Short drive."

The blue hospital gown for him was a fashion statement, the too-long sleeves of his XXXL apparel presenting opportunities for mischief. It was early spring in the small Idaho town, and the nurse had wheeled him out into the courtyard to enjoy the sunshine and to get a little fresh air. She stood beside him in case he needed anything. He looked up at her, and asked her if she would like to see stars. She said, "Well, sure, I guess so." He pointed his right arm straight at her, his arm pulled back into the too-long sleeve, holding the sleeve slightly open with his left hand, his right hand inside the sleeve balled into a fist, and said, "Look here into the opening of this sleeve, and I will help you see stars."

Humor contains two elements. One, as described above, is the element of surprise. You are led down one path, and suddenly the path takes a different direction. The other is the element of victim. Someone is surprised, annoyed, exposed or set up. In slapstick humor the victim is obvious, as they are physically assaulted, sometimes literally slapped with a stick. In other humor the mind or sensibility is assaulted, or one's view of reality is turned upside-down (surprise element).

During challenging times, when it appears that events are conspiring against us, humor can remind us to not take ourselves too seriously. Often this becomes self-deprecating humor. Self-deprecating humor is acceptable in Western culture, though not in all cultures. We can always find something

The Wisdom of K. Hieronymus

Beware the dark side of humor. Humor can be used as a weapon. Do not use sarcasm as a sword. Avoid humor at the expense of others. Mean-spirited humor is a misapplication of the power of mirth.

Avoid dirty jokes or bathroom humor. Such do not build nobility of character, nor cast you in a positive light. Walk the other way.

about ourselves to poke fun at. When the victim is ourselves, we do well to laugh liberally. Recognizing our foibles makes us human and keeps our feet on the ground. It can also help take the fear and the sting out of change.

Humor brings to mind better days past and future, and invites shared celebration. It reminds us that often what appeared as bad times resulted in good times. "Remember the time..." spoken at a gathering of family or friends is almost always a gateway to laughter.

Humor helps us deal with tragedy, with change that did not bring us what we were hoping for. It has long been recognized by playwrights that tragedy and comedy are two sides of the coin that is generated by the human experience.

To repeat a quote said during a time when our family was experiencing a car tragedy way beyond our anticipation, my father said, "If it weren't for bad luck, we wouldn't be having any luck at all."

My father also used to say that it is obvious that the Good Lord has a sense of humor, based on some of the creatures he has made (and some of the people).

There are different kinds of humor. Look for your favorite genre and it will speak to you. One genre I like is known as sick humor. For example:

Child — "But I like playing with grandma!"

Parent — "So help me, if you dig her up one more time!"

I also like **Will Rogers**'s cowboy humor:

"When you find yourself in a hole, stop digging!"

"Always drink from the stream uphill from the herd."

Almost all humor has something to offer by way of lightening our load and enhancing camaraderie.

APPLICATION
Employ this principle to benefit you and those you love

Humor is often portrayed in stories. Some people are natural storytellers. Others can learn to be. Skill in doing so comes from practice.

For example: I go on a fair number of backpacking trips, at least once every year for the last nine years. My friend Mike and I are about to embark on our 8th annual hike in the Wyoming Wind River mountains. We hope it will go better than a few years ago, when we decided to use horses to pack the bulk of our gear. This was a logical move, given the three-fold purpose of our adventure—camaraderie (with solitude as contrast), beauty (inspiration and photography), and FISHING. Optimal fishing in this case meant a rubber raft to row to the middle of the high mountain lakes, where the big ones are hunkered down and hungry. The rubber raft was very heavy—but no problem; horses are strong.

Unfortunately, the only horses we had available were designed by training and genetics to be endurance racing horses. Their names were Bob and Khalila (Arabian for flower). They did love to run. But in this case we wanted them to walk. With their reins in our hands trailing behind us as we walked the rugged trail, we were constantly slowing them down, so as not to be trodden upon. But they mostly behaved themselves well and got our gear to camp, deep in the mountains.

In camp, they became docile, grass-munching creatures. But the appearance of placidity turned out to be a ruse. It was all part of a plot that Bob and Khalila had hatched on the way up to lull us into a false sense of security.

The first morning we awoke to the drumbeat of galloping hooves, the sounds quickly becoming softer and softer in the distance. Mike grabbed a rope and sped over the hill after them. Travis and I followed. Fortunately the horses had the good sense to take the trail, so tracking them was easier. We followed the tracks for hours—one small set (Khalila), unshod, and one large set, shod (Bob).

Finally, in the distance, we saw our quarry. But they were the wrong color. Brown and black— not Bob, not Khalila. The tracks were the tracks that they would have and should have left, but were not. We had been tracking the wrong horses for hours. Somehow we found humor in the surprise.

During a short conference, we decided that they belonged to someone (brilliant), and that they would appreciate having them back, and that while we were looking for the rightful owner, they might as well haul our gear. Slight misjudgment, as it turned out.

I suppose you could say that we decided in that moment to become horse thieves. I preferred to think of it as horse borrowers, or even as "The Wyoming Good Samaritans" who were kind enough to take their precious time to return escaped horses to their rightful owners. We put the halter ropes on the new horses and set off back to camp.

Just then a shot rang out (just kidding). The forest was silent.

We finally got them back to camp. Mike saddled up to ride to the other side of the lake to ask the campers there, who had horses, if they knew the rightful owners. They pointed us in a direction that proved to be correct.

I imagined the rightful owners finding us with our gear strapped to their horses' backs, yanking out their lever-action Winchesters and ratcheting rounds into the chamber, muzzles pointed at our chests.

I played the fantasy dialogue in my mind. "But we were just borrowing them, sir—trying to find the rightful owner."

The response: "Speaking of what's right, you have the right to remain silent. In fact, I wish you would."

That dark fantasy did not come to pass. What did come to pass, at midmorning, halfway back to Moon Lake, was the horses getting spooked by something and bucking and kicking and strewing gear all over the mountainside. We never did find Mike's sleeping bag and he slept on the cold ground in his coat that night.

We finally did come across the rightful owners. They thanked us, promised to come back the next morning to help us haul our gear out, did not come back until too late (client emergency), and we ended up hauling out most of the gear on our backs, in two trips, leaving the raft and saddles behind, stashing them under a heap of pine boughs for later retrieval.

Someone found Khalila that evening wandering around the outskirts of town, and the authorities spotted Bob a week later wandering around the airport, hoping to sneak onto a flight to a warmer climate, we are quite sure.

Be ready to tell the humorous stories of your life. They will always be there. You will not have to look hard.

Humor has as many uses as there are shades of green: it can be used to deflect hurt, to cheer others, to reframe change, to attack others (biting humor), to nail insights (for example, my second-oldest son, in a moment of quiet reflection, saying he was "hatching plots against the day lilies," in our uphill campaign to eliminate same from our property). The lilies have really taken over in the last several years, and will likely win (this is a Type IV change, but the knowledge that humor makes any situation more bearable will help us persevere in coping with this change.

LIFE TOOLS™
Use consistently until they become your tools for life

1. If you have children, or nieces or nephews, start creating "funny cards." Funny cards are a record of things they say or do as they are growing up. Put them on index cards, or in a file on your computer's hard drive, along with the precise age of the child, and file them away. Find occasion later to read them. These are great things to haul out and read at birthday celebrations, just before cutting the cake, for example, especially if a girlfriend or boyfriend is in attendance.

2. Start a humor file in a drawer or a shelf in a bookcase or a place on your computer's hard drive—include quotes, pictures, stories, commentary— whatever strikes your funny bone. Share the humor with others. Humor grows greatly when shared.

3. Visit a bookstore. Peruse the titles in the humor section. Pick one that appeals to you. Read in it every day or so. Allow yourself to laugh out loud. If something is particularly funny, read it out loud to someone else.

4. Start telling jokes to family or friends. If this is a new behavior for you,

practice out loud as many times as needed to feel totally comfortable. Jerry Seinfeld practiced a few simple jokes dozens and dozens of times to prepare for the two minutes of opportunity on the Johnny Carson show that launched his career.

5.   Find humor in a challenging change that comes into your life. Let one of your first impulses be to laughter, not anger. Point out the humor to others.

6.   Make note of who you like to be around because of their sense of humor. Spend more time with them. Tell them how much you appreciate their sense of humor.

7.   A cheerful outlook and a sense of humor tend to go hand in hand. Cultivate a cheerful, optimistic outlook. Consciously point out the bright side of every situation. This is especially important during unexpected, negative change

8.   Tell stories that point to the absurdity of life. If this does not come naturally, start by sharing with a trusted person a simple account of what happened to you today. Note especially those things that surprised you or turned you to a new path.

TRAPS

Beware of thinking you have to be as funny as a professional comic before attempting to share anything humorous. Just start. You will learn as you go, and embarrassment will not be permanent. Push past clumsiness.

Don't think you have to find humor in every event. Humor in some circumstances is inappropriate.

As always, be ready for resistance as you change, from yourself and from others. Do not let the opposition of resistance stop you.

PERPETUAL ENCOURAGEMENT

When change comes, when the unexpected throws you off kilter, look for the humor.

Always look on the bright side, and on the light side.

Humor is the universal medicine, the main cure for pessimism, the antidote for the negative emotion caused by unwanted change. Humor and optimism will stride forward hand in hand.

As you become more cheerful and expressive of humor, you will attract positive, interesting people.

APPENDIX

There is truth in all humor. See humor as the pathway to insight; look for the truth, and act accordingly. For example, there is truth in the following:

"It's OK to let yourself go, as long as you can let yourself back." - Anonymous

"My advice is to start out slow, and then taper off from there." - **Walt Stack**

Famous last words of a redneck—"Hey fellas, watch this!" - **Jeff Foxworthy** (Guess who the victim is).

SUMMARY

1. Decide to cultivate the humorous side of life, the bright side. Cultivate a cheerful, positive outlook.

2. Start a humor file. Buy humorous books, write down stories, make a stack or a file of notes and clippings.

3. Consciously use humor as a life tool: to deflect hurt, to cheer others, to reframe change, to nail insights and to objectify tough events.

4. Respond to unexpected change, especially challenging, daunting change by looking for the humor.

5. Seek ways to share humor with others.

6. Be willing to tell stories on yourself. Note the funny things that happen to you each day and share the stories with others.

7. Do not succumb to the seduction of the dark side of humor—sarcasm, mean-spirited humor, or filthy jokes.

PRINCIPLE 12:

Exercise Stewardship

When change comes, do not try to control everything. Be conscious of what's in, what's out, what is your responsibility and within your control, what is not. Act strongly in your areas of responsibility, your stewardships. Magnify your opportunities. Keep your commitments. Do first things first. Prepare every needful thing. Keep track. Monitor a completions list.

SONGLINE
Learn to navigate the wilderness of change

In Biblical times, no man or woman was given more land than he or she was able to quicken. Then when the person mastered the production of that land (fulfilled his or her stewardship), more was given.

Likewise, by virtue of being alive, we are each given a field to cultivate. We do not often choose the field, and sometimes change chooses for us, but we always have choices. At the very least, we may choose in what manner to take it on, to fulfill the opportunity. When we master that opportunity, the natural human tendency is to want to take on more.

When I was sixteen, I was given a responsibility to bring together a community of people into a common cause. I had helpers and precedents, but I was the point person. I remember how embracing that opportunity brought me joy. I had never done anything like it before; I had never been entrusted with that much. I did not accomplish all that could have been accomplished, but I did all that I could accomplish. The memory continues to sustain me.

Stewardship comprises four things: trust, resources, action and accountability.

First, we are entrusted with doing something new in our world.

Second, we are provided the resources (or we obtain them) necessary to fulfill the trust—this may include research, the labor of others, or advice and support from one who is wiser.

Third, we take action.

Fourth, we must at some point return and report. We must give an account of our stewardship.

I was recently privileged to participate with an accomplished group of 24 young people, who were examining their professional lives, and planning for the next phase. I was their teacher, but they taught me. Which is often the case. One woman in the group, speaking on the basis of her past success, said of previous pursuits: "I have learned to find something interesting in everything I do."

The story is told of a woman who had a very boring job. She was a kitchen helper for a wealthy landowner. Her job was to peel potatoes, all day every day. This was her stewardship. As she sat on the back porch, bemoaning her fate, a certain philosopher passed by. He asked her what was bothering her. She described the utter boredom of her task. He listened patiently, then pointed at the string of ants that were marching in and out of the house, bearing crumbs of food. He asked her how much she knew about ants—their habits, their characteristics, their communal structure. He challenged her to use a part of her attention in exploring the subject, as the other part of her mind continued to peel the potatoes.

She took on his challenge. She began to notice the pattern of the ants' movements. She became so intrigued that she hurried to the library after her day's work was done, and read as much as she could. She followed the march of the ants to

The Wisdom of K. Hieronymus

Do not wait for a stewardship to be given to you. Be like a child. Let yourself be possessed of an explorer's mind. Look for interesting subjects and things to tackle.

Cultivate personal curiosity and ask questions. Do not wait for permission nor social approval.

Do not accept a stewardship that does not serve and edify. Many throughout history have been offered stewardships of destruction, by evil and designing men and women. Sadly, some have accepted. Do not be one of them.

their home, and studied the interactions. She noticed there was a complex differentiation and social structure. She began to record her findings. From time to time, the philosopher would come by and ask her questions to point her in new directions. She became engrossed in her subject, even as she continued to create mounds and mounds of potato peelings.

After many months, she had compiled an impressive set of descriptions of the ant community, and acquired a prodigious amount of knowledge from her reading. She learned there were many kinds of ants, and branched out in her spare time to study them. The philosopher helped her to compile her writings into book format, and she was able to publish a small volume. Soon she found herself giving lectures and teaching seminars. She became recognized as a foremost expert. After she had exhausted the topic of ants, she became interested in the beetles she noticed at the doorstep, and followed a similar course. After a few years, the potato peelings were a thing of the past, and she had become recognized as a prominent expert and teacher. She continued to learn for the rest of her life. She had fulfilled and magnified her stewardship.

This woman was in the best of all stewardship conditions: she was fulfilling a stewardship that she had created herself, and was doing something that she enjoyed and was good at.

Of equal value is fulfilling a stewardship that has been given by another that you have made your own by embracing it.

All subjects are worthy of careful stewardship; there are no uninteresting subjects, just uninterested people.

APPLICATION
Employ this principle to benefit you and those you love

Stewardship is defined as the careful and responsible management of something entrusted to one's care .

We all have stewardships. They can be grand; they can be small.

Focusing on stewardship makes us a solid piece of the landscape even as change swirls around us.

Every day is an opportunity to contribute, to do something, however small, in our personal sphere, to tidy up our little corner of the world. You can learn to relish these opportunities. And even to create them.

Jonah, when called to teach hard truths to the inhabitants of Nineveh, worked hard to avoid his stewardship. It found him anyway. And with the merest of efforts, he succeeded in fulfilling it.

Do not try to avoid yours, or you might find yourself engulfed in a stream of circumstances that propel you into a dark time only to spew you out onto the edge of your task. This is often the function of unexpected, unwelcome change. It serves as a reset button.

We can start by describing our stewardships. They will likely fall into three main categories:

> **Family:** What does my family need from me right now? What will success in my family look like long term?

> **Work:** What can I uniquely accomplish in my work? Who depends on me

to do my part, and what do they need?

Personal: What are my interests? What are my passions and desires?

Stewardship begins when you make an offer to provide something to others at large. Sometimes this looks like volunteering. Sometimes it looks like a trade. Sometimes it looks like a job.

Be exacting and diligent in fulfilling those things that have been entrusted to you.

State clearly what you will do, by when, and how will you will measure, track, and report progress.

Being conscious of your stewardships provides you an anchor, an avenue of stability and familiarity in times of change.

Some opportunities, or proffered stewardships, can appear to be undesirable. You might find yourself strongly resisting. You could feel fear or trepidation or nervousness or anxiety. Paradoxically, this may be a sign that you should accept and proceed with the opportunity. The universe might be calling for you to experience personal growth, to increase your change resilience. This acceptance ultimately leads to peace.

On the other hand, such feelings, especially if there is a darkness to them, may be signals that you are to walk away. Through exercising choice and taking action, you will learn to discern.

Sometimes you will have to defend your stewardship. Stand ready to do so. This is your territory. You have claimed it, earned it, and you deserve to keep it.

Examples from two of my great uncles:

> Uncle Ed was a barber. That was his stewardship. He gave me my first haircut. But it was far from his first. He cut hair for years out of his little shop in Oakley, Idaho. Sometimes for very rough characters. One day an unkempt cowboy came into town after a long stint out on the open range, announced he wanted a shave and a haircut, settled himself into the chair, pulled out his six shooter and pulled back the hammer. He set it on the chair next to his right hand, and said, "One slip!" Ed proceeded to nonchalantly cut his hair and administered a close shave. The customers seated in the chairs waiting their turn were very attentive during this process. When the cowboy had left, one of them asked Ed if he had been nervous.

He said, "Not at all; I had that razor close to his throat the entire time." I have no doubt who would have won that confrontation. Ed would have retained his stewardship.

The other uncle was out working in the potato fields, near Oakley. He set the water running through the furrows, then laid down on his back in the shade for a quick nap while the water soaked to the end of the field, before switching it to another part of the property. He fell asleep.

He awoke suddenly, aware of a heavy weight on his chest and a buzzing in his ears, and slowly opened his eyes to find himself looking eye to eye with a diamondback rattler, coiled on his chest. My uncle calmly sized up the situation, then made a sudden move with his left hand (no other part of his body moved) to grip the snake tightly just below the poison sacks. Then he slowly drew his revolver from the holster at his right side, took careful aim, squeezed the trigger, and what had been a snake became a snake with no head. The buzzing stopped.

No one can take from you what is yours. Do not let them.

LIFE TOOLS™
Use consistently until they become your tools for life

1. Help others fulfill their stewardships—be bold enough to ask them what they will do by when, and how they will report progress.

2. One way to focus on stewardship is to list the roles you currently fulfill in life. For me it would be son, brother, teacher, leader, genealogist, outdoor athlete. Then give yourself a grade on how you are doing. Try to assess your performance in terms of what the potential recipients of your stewardship would say. Rate yourself high, medium or low. This is not to induce guilt, but rather to sort out priorities. As you do this, needed actions will come to mind. What are they?

3. Someone is the customer of your work stewardship. Someone needs and expects what you are fulfilling. Who is that person? Write down their name and write down what they need or expect from you.

4. Ask a friend what they believe, just from watching you, knowing you, listening to you, what they would say are your main priorities. See if you agree.

5. Use your skills from the fulfillment module to map out a plan in an area of stewardship. It does not have to be complex.

6. If you are married, ask your spouse how well you are providing for them the things the hope for and expect from you. Do not accept their first kind or cautious answer. Continue to probe. Give them some starter ideas, if needed.

7. Read the parables of the talents. There are several versions. Meditate on the words. Look your fears in the face, and do something different next time.

8. Look back over the change resilience skills you have practiced and strengthened thus far in this program. Which can you pull out, reapply, and exercise in the tasks at hand?

9. Surprise someone. Volunteer for a dirty job that no one else wants. Fulfill it impeccably.

TRAPS

Motive is everything. Do not be seduced by a stewardship that offers only personal gratification or praise from others. Rather, seek opportunities to serve. Ask yourself: "What's in it for others?"

Don't make assumptions; don't take things personally.

PERPETUAL ENCOURAGEMENT

Be thankful for problems and challenges. Without them, life would be boring. There would be no work, no growth, no meaning, no joy. And no stewardship.

Peace and joy come from making and keeping commitments to yourself.

Do not be afraid to stretch yourself. Life is designed to stretch us. You can accomplish many things that you do not now believe to be possible.

APPENDIX

Stewardship is performed by a steward. Other words for steward are: agent, manager, broker, implementer, expediter, facilitator, functionary, envoy, operative, delegate, servant, attendant, trustee. Which ones are you?

"In times of rapid change, experience is our worst enemy." - **J. Paul Getty**

SUMMARY

1. Adult lives consist of stewardships.

2. Stewardship is the careful and responsible management of something entrusted to one's care.

3. Fulfilling our stewardships brings joy and peace.

4. Stewardships consist of four things: trust, resources, action, and accountability. Pay attention to all four and design your stewardships accordingly:

   - We are entrusted with doing something new in our world.

   - We are provided the resources (or we obtain them) necessary to fulfill the trust—this may include research, the labor of others or advice and support from one who is wiser.

   - We take action.

   - We must at some point return and report. We must give an account of our stewardship actions.

PRINCIPLE 13:

Invent Projects

Invent projects to focus energy and to resist the distraction of change challenges. See yourself as the project manager. Fasten your mind on the end benefits of the project. Apply the power of projects to bring together the principles of fulfillment structures, the drive to closure and stewardship—in planning, action, contribution and completion. When finished, declare success, then move quickly to the next worthy project. Close, acknowledge, celebrate, rejoice, mobilize, and move on.

SONGLINE
Learn to navigate the wilderness of change

A project has an objective (results, milestones, and deliverables), accountability, set-aside resources (time, money and other resources such as knowledge and committed help from others), a launch sequence, quality and "customer" and progress measures, and an end point.

A project can be as simple or complex as writing a paper, mopping the kitchen floor, servicing the car, painting the bathroom, repairing a machine, washing the windows, selecting an item of outdoor gear, polishing the car, organizing furniture, preparing for and completing a bike race, finishing the laundry, processing all emails in your inbox, teaching a sewing skill, writing a poem, finishing a painting, building a website, teaching a child a new skill, hanging a hummingbird feeder, creating a family photography album, designing a class, planting the flowerbeds, organizing a bridal shower, finishing a brochure.

A project can be as time-consuming as organizing a class reunion, finishing a skyscraper that takes many years, rebuilding an athletic team over a period of time, completing a college degree or earning a certificate or achieving Eagle Scout status, designing a new line of automobiles, or achieving one's 40 year wedding anniversary.

Or it could be achieving success after success as an Idaho potato farmer: **Delmar Mecham** could grow potatoes like no other. He turned himself into someone who could produce winning harvest after winning harvest. He was very close to the soil. In fact, I saw him more than once, when surveying plants in progress, reach down, take a pinch of soil, and place it on this tongue as if he were a master chef testing the broth before adding more ingredients. He would roll the soil over his taste buds, then make a decision whether it was time for more fertilizer, more water, less water.

The four of us, his sun-burnished, teenaged, bare-chested farmhands, then looked to him for pronouncement. We hung on his words because they defined our lives. He would tell us what would be done over the next days and months to bring the crop to maximum fruition. We did not know it, but he was inventing projects for us.

Projects have a beginning (conception and launch), a middle (focused effort and persistent application of inputs), and an end (quality check, wrap-up, celebration and handoff to the end user—which could be ourselves). Then on to the next project.

Thinking of life this way takes us off the treadmill of tedium. It creates endpoints and motivation. It keeps us focused and productive.

Projects create a stable, contributive path through the onslaught of change and distraction.

The principle of inventing projects ties together earlier principles of embracing stewardship, creating fulfillment structures, and driving closure. It is where all of these come together in action, contribution, and completion.

Inventing projects is an act of creation. Inventing and completing projects creates the lasting and worthwhile stuff of our lives.

I once was in a role where I led the completion of project

The Wisdom of K. Hieronymus

When tackling a project:

Expect volunteers. Look for others to come forward and help.

Volunteers are sometimes (often?) an annoyance. They interrupt the smooth flow of how we think things should occur. Yet volunteers often offer something that is missing. We might feel criticized as we realize the gap or personal weakness that is revealed. Or, we might be put off or become nervous because they are not doing things our way. That is good, because there is not always time for us to do it our way, and sometimes our way will not work.

Encourage, welcome, and embrace any and all help.

That said, it will not always work out and we might need to invite them to disengage. But often it does work.

---

after project after project. Usually this consisted of working with a project leader from another entity, coaching and leading them through the launch, progress, and completion of the project.

There came a point in each project where the other person took on the burden.

I could feel it and see it in the seriousness of their face, as if they had just realized the extent of what they had on their hands, and had accepted the reality that completion was in their hands. They would sometimes get cranky, get scared, or begin to make unreasonable demands on me or level unjust criticism at me. I just rode it out, and soon the time would pass, they would relax, become reconciled to what needed to be done, dig in and move forward. They began to ask the right questions, and make the right requests of me. It was always a sweet moment for me, and a relief. At that moment, I became confident that the work would be accomplished.

Most of you will go through this emotional evolution as you truly take on a project of importance.

APPLICATION
Employ this principle to benefit you and those you love

When inventing a project, begin with both the middle and the end in mind. Pay attention to sudden strokes of ideas as you write out a plan.

The word "invent" was invented in the 1400's in Middle English. It derives from the Latin "inventus," which means to come upon or find. The archaic meaning is "to discover." Other meanings are: to devise by thinking, to fabricate, to produce (as something useful) for the first time through the use of the imagination or by ingenious thinking and experiment.

The best inventions are often simple. Invention starts with focused thought, or even with daydreaming, about things that would bring benefit or help you accomplish your goals and serve others. It proceeds with experimentation, or trying things out and learning from mistakes.

To invent a project means to tinker and try something that solves a problem or addresses a future hope (although all hopes are future-oriented, I have used the word "future" to emphasize the importance of forward thinking). Then at some point, to invent a project means to transition to an organized, structured approach.

Opportunities for projects are discovered by thinking about what is important to you. You may endlessly distract yourself with television, half-listening to the entertaining but vapid broadcasts. Or, you can "explore" in terms of what you and others need to improve your lives. You can keep a steady course of interest, excitement, or contribution even as change swirls around you.

Thinking in terms of projects keeps you unwavering in the face of change.

Think of yourself as a project manager. A project manager has three main responsibilities:

- Keep both the middle and the end in mind.
- Keep things on track by asking questions of yourself and others.
- Bring closure, recognition, and celebration.

Set out a visual reminder or structure that will keep you focused and mindful of what it is you are accomplishing. This can be an excel spreadsheet, a sequential list, or a table with three parts—who will do what by when. Or you might use some other creative method. For example, an artist I know lays out a "connected collage." arranged and sequenced according to the timing and steps of the creative challenge she has given herself.

Most projects benefit from holding a kickoff meeting. A kickoff meeting provides five things:

- Introduces the players and their roles
- Makes sure everyone understands the mission
- Sets the standard
- Sets timeframes for milestones, deliverables and completion, and stablishes patterns of communication and decision-making

Not everything needs to be a project. Just pick the important things. And as you approach the important things in life as a series of projects (inventing and completing), you begin to think more productively in general, and become more focused and effective. You will make productive use of change energy.

Every project has a customer, an end user. The customer might be yourself, it might be an individual or a group. Work to your customer's requirements.

Ask these 15 questions during the course of a project:

1. **Conception:** Which possibilities should we most strongly focus on?
2. **Customers:** Who are we doing this for (self, which others...)?
3. **Preparation:** What resources must be secured and what agreements put in place and what change be incorporated to insure success?
4. **Cost:** What budget do we have to work with?
5. **Team:** Who needs to be on the project team?

6. **Schedule:** What is our timeframe?

7. **Safety:** How do we keep everyone safe, both physically and emotionally?

8. **Measurement:** How do we measure progress and final success?

9. **Quality:** What are our quality standards?

10. **Partners:** Who outside the project team will help make it happen?

11. **Action:** What are the first steps?

12. **Re-conception:** At this stage, knowing what we have learned, what adjustments do we need to make?

13. **Completion:** What change do we want to consolidate and how do we wrap things up?

14. **Lessons learned:** What lessons can we apply to other projects?

15. **Celebration:** How can we acknowledge contribution and rejoice together?

LIFE TOOLS™
Use consistently until they become your tools for life

1. One of the best project analysis and planning structures is a simple five-column table. The first column is for the "who." The second is for the "what". The third is for the "by when." The fourth is for "how progress will be measured". The fifth is for "comments." Comments are things to keep in mind, such as quality measures, how success will be evaluated, who else needs to buy in. Use this structure to map out something that you are planning to accomplish.

2. Make a list of your current projects or goals. List the people you hope will volunteer to help. Seek them out. Tell them about the project, what you hope for as an outcome, and why it is important to you. Notice what happens. If anyone offers to help, you have just secured a volunteer.

3. Make a list of recent Type IV changes (unwelcome, unanticipated) in your life. Invent a project in the face of these changes to harness the energy and move you in a desired direction. Other types of changes are also candidates.

4. Focus on the middle and also on the end point of a current important project. Cut pictures out of magazines or the newspaper or print things

off the web to create a collage that represents both the middle and the completion of the project. Place it in a prominent place where you will see it often.

5. List or think of a current project. Ask the 15 questions.

6. For one of your projects that involves other people (even if it is just one other person), hold a kickoff meeting. Accomplish the five objectives. A kickoff meeting may also be done even if you are the only person doing the project.

7. Look back over the change-resilience skills you have practiced and strengthened thus far in this change energy adventure. Which can you pull out and focus on the projects you have on your hands?

8. Surprise someone. Volunteer to help with someone else's project. Especially look for opportunities to manage events through change. Fulfill your role impeccably. If the opportunity presents itself, share some of the principles in this module.

TRAPS

Motive is paramount. Do not be seduced by a project that offers only personal gratification or praise of others. Rather, seek opportunities to serve. Ask yourself: "What's in it for others"?

Don't make assumptions. Check things out.

Don't take things personally. Think from the perspective of the other person's reality.

You might feel a tendency to let up towards the end of a project, right when it is almost complete. Push through to completion. Clean and put away the tools, do the paperwork.

PERPETUAL ENCOURAGEMENT

Be thankful for projects. Without them, life would not progress. There would be no growth, no meaning, no service, no joy. And no accomplishment.

Think vision, execution, summation, celebration.

Peace and joy come from making and keeping commitments to yourself.

Do not wait until your project is completed to perfection to ship it. Declare it complete, turn it over, move on. A project done satisfactorily, finished, is better than a project done perfectly, unfinished.

APPENDIX

"Concerning all acts of initiative and creation, there is one elementary truth—that the moment one definitely commits oneself, then Providence moves, too."
- **W. H. Murray**, The Story of Everest

Invention (for example, of projects) stems not just from genius, but from persistence. "Obstacles cannot crush me. Every obstacle yields to stern resolve." - **Leonardo da Vinci**

SUMMARY

1. Thinking of your life in terms of projects helps you maintain a sense of engagement, accomplishment, and completion. It also improves the quality of your work.

2. Projects have a beginning, a middle, and an end. Each stage has different requirements and mindsets. Keep all three in mind.

3. Kickoff meetings are beneficial at the beginning of most projects, even if the meeting is only with yourself. Kickoff meetings accomplish five things. They: introduce the players and their roles, make sure the players all understand the mission, set the standard, set timeframes for milestones, deliverables, and completion, and establish patterns of communication and decision-making.

4. 15 questions put "muscle" behind every project (see above under "application").

5. Every change, no matter the type, creates energy and the opportunity for the invention of a project.

6. One of the most neglected parts of any project is celebration of completion and acknowledgement of the players.

7. Approaching life as a series of projects, with ourselves as the project manager, makes us more change resilient.

PRINCIPLE 14:

Nurture Positive Relationships

Positive relationships, like well-trimmed sails on a ship, will carry you safely through the storms of change. Be open to meeting new people. Seek people who edify and build up. Spend more time with people who encourage. Spend less time with those who discourage. Depart from those who are constantly critical. Flee toxic relationships and make more time for positive relationships.

SONGLINE
Learn to navigate the wilderness of change

To be alive is to have relationships. Some relationships are negative, some are positive. All relationships have potential to teach; all have potential to be positive. All of your relationships have potential to stunt your change resilience; all have potential to enhance your change resilience.

When I was a freshman in college, in a large and strange city, I went through a period of homesickness. The tall structures of New York City were not like the tall structures of the Rocky Mountains, where I was from. A number of other people were in New York, for schooling and for other reasons, who were from my part of the world. One time in particular, I sat in a class at church, and began talking to the person next to me, who was five or six years older than I, also from the Rockies. This was our initial connection. He asked me how things were going. As I spoke, he must have sensed my mood.

He put his arm around me, and said nothing in particular, but gave me the reassurance that I had a friend whenever I needed one.

It was a simple gesture of support, but that relationship and resultant reassurance carried me through that time of Type 1 (expected, welcome) change and dislocation.

Wherever there are people, this force for good is available.

I often envy the deer I see eating the leaves on our cliff-side property behind our house. A wealth of nourishment surrounds them. They eat seemingly at random, but I know they are being selective. Thus it is with us. A wealth of potential nourishment surrounds us in the form of potential relationships. We may choose to partake of the positive, we may indulge in the negative, or we may choose to eat not at all. Partaking of the positive relationships enlarges our understanding, the strength of our being-in-the-world, and carries us through the storms of change.

There are some people with whom we instantly strike up rapport. They are a lot like us. We are simpatico. These relationships tend to endure for a long time. There are others with whom the rapport is not so instant.

When we were in the hospital, in labor with our youngest, there was another couple also pacing the hallway. She and my wife had the same doctor. The other couple's baby came just before ours, and the doctor had to rush, just in time, to deliver ours. We thought nothing more of it. Then, a few months later, we walked into church on a Sunday morning, and saw a couple sitting on the back row, with a baby about the same age as ours. They looked familiar. Then it struck us. They were the couple that had been in the hospital at the same time. Recognition sparked with all of us and we exchanged warm greetings.

Her name was Toni. We learned that Toni's father had the distinction of being the only professional football quarterback who had Super Bowl rings from both the Canadian and the American football leagues. Toni, (Detroit-born), was much more outspoken than my wife and she had her own very strong opinions that she was not afraid to voice. Lin (Virginia-born) was southern-gentle and quiet. Polar opposites.

The Wisdom of K. Hieronymus

Some relationships will challenge you. They may create stress or trigger negative feelings. They are what are commonly called "difficult relationships." The temptation is to move on, or even to stonewall.

In many cases moving on is exactly the right path. But in other cases, exiting will cause you to miss an opportunity for learning and growth. The people in the relationship may have come into your life as your teachers. Take a moment to reflect on what you have to learn, how you have to change for the relationship to work. Name the trait. Is this something you are striving to learn? If the answer is yes, embrace the learning opportunity.

As Lin says, "I thought that we could probably never be good friends, as much because of my soft spoken ways as because of her more outspoken ways."

But something happened—within months they had become fast friends. It started out quietly, and in small ways, talking about children, talking about life and choices and struggles, finding humor in the foibles of others, including some of my foibles. They developed rapport of the heart.

They did not close the door on each other before the relationship had opportunity to blossom. They invested in the relationship. They brought honesty and balance into each other's lives. They became best friends.

All encounters with other people present opportunities for relationships. Some will be deep and lasting such as [examples]; some will be marginal and fleeting, like the interchange with the volunteer leader who teaches us a new skill, or with the trucker who stops to administer roadside help. You possess the divine endowment to choose how you invest so that a relationship is either enlarged or diminished.

Each of us experiences the world in our own unique way. We find things that we enjoy, foods we don't like, we notice we have picked a favorite color. Likewise, we create relationships in our own way. You need to discover and honor your way.

Sometimes parents and children don't get along. For decades. Or for life. However, there is always a relationship. Applying the principles of this Personal Change Resilience Methodology increases your capacity to reinvent troubling relationships so that they are less deadening and more enlivening.

APPLICATION
Employ this principle to benefit you and those you love

Relationships are part of how we learn, how we get our start in life, how we discover who we are. Relationships are pathways to the expansion of our personalities; they are lifelines to our future. Relationships are a crucial part of our journey along the road of personal change resilience.

People employ different styles in forming relationships. Many are extroverts. They have "never met a stranger." To them, everyone is interesting, everyone merits a smile and an open heart, everyone is a candidate for lifelong relationship.

However, one third of the people in the United States, probably in the world, are not like that. Instead, they are introverts. Introverts take stock of what is around them, processing information internally, measuring the impact of potential actions before moving forward or advancing the relationship. This can be a handicap in the early stages of a relationship. On the other hand, introverts make some of the best friends—once they decide to be your friend, they invest heavily and are often friends for life.

But introverts, like all minorities, must recognize that the onus of building a bridge to others is in their hands, not the hands of others. In most cases, it serves them to choose to act like the majority, the extroverts. And even extroverts can have introvert moments, or even weeks, and must consciously reach out and for relationships.

Introverts can watch extroverts and "take notes." They can learn an important change resilience skill—how to cultivate relationship with another, at will. At will means once you decide you want a relationship, you are able to strike it up, like striking up a match. You are able to convey openness, positive regard, and give and take. And boundaries.

There are risks in all relationships. Once we reveal ourselves to another, we put ourselves in a situation where we might be hurt or disappointed . But there is no real growth without the investment of risk.

Take risk. Step up and out of your comfort zone. Invest in new behavior. Building personal change resilience requires investment. When we invest, we put something at risk.

There are four prime ways to create relationship. Use what works best for you:

- Do work, or projects, with another. Rather than talk about how the relationship could be better, or about going to lunch, or getting to know someone better, take action, start a project, invite partnership and produce something useful together.

- Give experiential feedback to another (neither positive or negative, just how you are experiencing the other person). Do this by saying something like, "This is how you come across to me...," or "This is what I think you are saying."

- Employ humor as a way to form bonds with others. Sometimes we refer to humor as a way to "break the ice."

- There is still another way. If humor is a way to break the ice, then asking sincere and relevant questions, and listening attentively to the answers, is a way to melt the ice.

Ask questions, then listen with interest to the answer. This takes away the reserve and sense of self-preservation that people possess.

Revealing something about yourself as a precursor to asking a question is often a great lead-in. Especially if it is something personal. You can talk about observations of things "in the past, out there." Or you can talk about feelings and observations "right now, right here, in here." The former is small talk; the latter is relationship.

All relationship, especially the initial and conversational part of relationship, is like improvisational comedy—each action makes a point and creates the next opening for action.

For example, instead of engaging in this type of dialogue: Joe—"I was walking down the street the other day and saw my mother-in-law coming the other way." Moe—"I hate talking to my mother-in-law." End of interaction.

Use this type: Joe—"I was walking down the street the other day and saw my mother-in-law." Moe—"Did she recognize you?" Joe now has an opening.

Pride inhibits relationships; humility nurtures relationships. Some decide that they need to be superior to be whole, that they need to achieve beyond the accomplishments of peers in order to be OK. This is the path of pride. Others decide that they are in the human mix to be taught and nourished, and in turn to teach and nourish. This is the path of humility and strength.

We experience times to plant, times to harvest, times to let lie dormant. Sometimes we need to cease investing in a relationship, and come back to it later. Sometimes we need to try something new. And some relationships simply cannot be fixed. At least for the moment. My rule of thumb is: try twice.

LIFE TOOLS™
Use consistently until they become your tools for life

1. In the next three weeks, reach out and form at least one new relationship.

2. Learn the skill of starting a conversation. Learn what to say after you say hello. Some call this small talk and think the impact is frivolous. But small talk becomes large talk. It can grow into significance. Take it on as a project. We always have at least one thing in common with another person. Asking them where they are from, what they are up to, what they have been doing, and learning more of their likes and dislikes in most cases ignites a highly intriguing interaction.

3. Take inventory of the relationships in your life. Make a list of those you wish to improve. Write down the first step. Push through fear or hesitation.

4.   Here are three standby questions: Have you read any good books lately? What's new with you? What are you up to these days? Try them.

5.   When a learner is ready, a teacher appears. Write down what you are ready (desirous) to learn. The teacher will likely appear, and bring occasion for a new relationship.

6.   There are four main sources of relationship opportunity: family, work, interpersonal, and accidental (just running into people). For one day, pay attention to all four. Notice what happens.

7.   People have different styles in forming relationships.

- Some, by serving.
- Some, by being served.
- Some, by teaching.
- Some, by being taught.
- Some, by diligently doing their job.

Identify your personal style and do it on purpose.

8.   Write down names of people who intrigue you or with whom you might want a closer relationship. Take the first step. Reach out and start a conversation.

TRAPS

Being in a relationship does not mean being in complete agreement. Being nice all the time is a sure path to shallow and short-lived relationships.

Your first try could fail or fall short. Don't give up after the first failed attempt. First efforts can be discouraging. New behavior is awkward and does not always work the first time. Try twice.

PERPETUAL ENCOURAGEMENT

Try new things. You can always shift if what you try does not work. You learn from anything new that you attempt.

For an enjoyable way to observe and learn the cycle of toxic relationship disengagement, watch the Sandra Bullock movie 28 Days.

APPENDIX

"No one can make you feel inferior without your permission." - **Eleanor Roosevelt**

"Feed opportunities; starve problems." - **Gordon B. Hinckley**. This is especially true of relationships.

"If you would go speedily, go alone. If you would go far, go as a group." - African proverb

Relationships are one of the two things that you will carry with you always. No one can take them away. The other thing is knowledge. This is the eternal dyad of personal change resilience.

Be a positive and enjoyable person to be around.

SUMMARY

1. Nurturing positive relationships carries you safely through the storms of change and builds personal change resilience.

2. Opportunities for positive relationship surround you on all hands.

3. Be open to relationships with people who at first may seem to be your opposite. They may teach us, stretch us and enliven us.

4. Some relationships are quite negative, yet inescapable, such as with some parents, siblings, or those who have contributed to hurtful or even traumatic experiences. We must acknowledge that these relationships are also part of our life, and make the most of them.

5. Discover and honor your own unique way of "doing relationships," and then more actively do it on purpose.

6. Flee toxic relationships.

7. Introverts can learn from extroverts how to reach out and form relationships.

8. There are four prime ways to develop relationships:

    • Do work, or projects, with another. Start a project, invite partnership and produce something useful together. Sports qualify. So do hobbies.

    • Give experiential feedback to another (neither positive or negative, just describe how you are experiencing the other person).

    • Employ humor as a way to form bonds with others.

    • Ask sincere and relevant questions, and listen attentively to the answers. This takes away the reserve and sense of self-preservation that people possess. Talk about feelings and observations that exist "right now, right here, in here".

9. Employ the principles of improvisational comedy to relationships. Do not cut off conversation. Always leave an opening for the other person.

10. Beware of the barrier of pride and pursue the strength of humility.

11. Know when to stop trying. Postpone relationship building until the time is right. At the same time, continually be an enjoyable person to be around.

PRINCIPLE 15:

Create Threads Of Stability

Threads of stability are self-created routines and rituals that comprise consistent daily, weekly, and monthly activities to carry and sustain us through change. They are especially important during unexpected and unwelcome change. These threads are the rhythms and underpinnings for our lives, created during times of need or clarity to provide scaffolding for our daily, weekly, monthly, and year-by-year well-being and progress. They cause constancy amid change. They feed our soul and spirit.

SONGLINE
Learn to navigate the wilderness of change

When I was 17 years old, I discovered a book that was electrifyingly inspirational. I read it cover to cover over that summer. It changed my life. Or rather, through the book's influence on my decision-making and faith and courage and relationships, my life was changed. Shortly thereafter, I made the reading of this book a thread of stability, or routine. I read it at least once every year. I still find new things, take notes and I follow through. I have read it 49 times.

Contrary to what has been said by some, you can go home again. No matter where you find yourself, routine can become your home and refuge.

Positive routines fill in gaps in motivation and clarity and carry you through rough times. They create a go-to place, a home base or home room for reestablishing focus and direction. They can be embodied in a practice, a person, or a place.

They establish a platform from which to absorb and repurpose the energy of change. They carry you in positive trim over the speed bumps of change.

Routines are like a pattern of strong threads woven into the cloth of our life, much like ripstop nylon fabric, which is woven with a double thread at regular intervals so that small tears do not spread. One example of a positive routine is the daily action of my former friend and mentor, who always took time to read the daily newspaper upon arriving home from work, which he decided to do because while he was growing up, his alcoholic father never had time for anything like that. This practice relaxed and refreshed him and provided a positive segue into the rest of the evening. Another example is the commitment of the owner of a company I once worked for, who had fresh flowers brought in every week for all the administrative assistants in the office.

Other examples of rituals and routines that create ripstop threads that keep small tears from becoming massive rips: The morning cup of coffee. The morning dose of CNN or FOX news. The weekly phone call to our parents. Arriving at work at the same hour. Getting in touch with customers on a routine basis.

Choose your routines wisely. A healthy routine has continuing positive impact. It can have immense impact on your physical or emotional well-being, your knowledge, your relationships. Some routines do not have to be chosen—they are already there. Find, relish, and wisely exploit the constants that already exist in your life.

I have learned how to make ritual serve me well. One year ago, I had never written a book. I had thought about writing a book, I had talked about writing a book, I had helped write books, written articles, white papers, manuals, proposals, but never engaged in the obdurate, long-term discipline of personally completing the entire body of work called "book."

Then I established a thread of stability, or routine, that I invoke for my professional writing. Here it is:

Every weekday I arise between 4:30 and 5:30 AM. (I should probably add that the routine

The Wisdom of K. Hieronymus

If you are not alert, routines can become ruts. A rut has been defined as a grave that is open at both ends. Examine your routines periodically to make sure they are not encasing you in old and non-productive habits. Perhaps the comfort of routine has become the confinement of indolence. Sometimes you will just know a change is in order—you will feel stuck, stagnant, and bored. When this feeling comes, make the change to a new set of habits—establish a new and edifying thread of stability.

___

actually starts the night before, with my going to bed sometime between 9:30 and 10:30 PM). I stretch. I put on comfortable clothing of warmth appropriate to the season. I shuffle down to my A-space in the basement. ("A" stands for "Alpha"— I swear this moniker was my wife's creation; she swears it wasn't). I sit on my southwest-design couch, read scripture, mark key passages, meditate, pray, and write down decisions for the day and week.

I pay close attention to thoughts that come to me. Then I put my scriptures away, roll my chair over to the desk sitting against the east wall under the window, fire up my computer and find the right document, position my two scented candles just so, left and right, strike the match and light them, put away the matches, carefully choose my inspiration rocks for the day from amongst the stash in the upper right hand corner of my desk (including the cube of fluorite from Madagascar, the small green rock I found on the shores of Lake Superior, the polished purplish-beige flint that I found at Enchanted Rock State Park in Texas, that my grandson "borrowed" and that came back into my possession months later, my beautiful sphere of jasper, etc.) where they have been radiating diverse strength into one another all night, position them just so next to my keyboard, always a new combination, so that their timeless solidity and creative synergy can flow into my hands.

I turn over the small, salmon-colored piece of paper that has the words printed on it — WHAT DOES THIS HAVE TO DO WITH WELCOMING CHANGE AND TURNING BAD TIMES INTO GOOD TIMES?, then I cup both hands and pull both candle scents simultaneously towards my nostrils. As the scents creatively combine into my awareness, I write the first word, then the second word. Then I am off and running. One year later, this thread of stability has delivered a book into my outstretched hands.

There is actually a bit more to the method. When I am really on my game, on Mondays, Wednesdays, and Fridays I do something called morning pages, an exercise that focuses all the senses into tight focus on one visceral image. I pulled this practice from a book on writing song lyrics. I use it to warm up my mind so I can write a bit more lyrically. On Tuesdays and Thursdays I spend 10 minutes visually exploring an earth-life goals collage. Then I write. All the above has become a ritual that invokes creativity and production.

APPLICATION
Employ this principle to benefit you and those you love

Several areas of your life will benefit from stability threads. These include but are not limited to relationships, knowledge, and physical and emotional well-being.

Some examples are:

- In the realm of relationships, you might agree to spend time with certain (edifying) people at a certain place every year.

- In the realm of knowledge, you can read a certain inspirational book as a matter of habit on a periodic basis. Or you can visit a certain website, or take in the daily news (beware excess negativity).

- In the realm of physical well-being, you can establish a regimen of fitness, perhaps paying someone to be your personal coach, or agreeing with a group of fellow exercisers to meet at certain times during the week.

- In the realm of emotional well-being, you can establish a habit of daily meditation.

All of these threads build your change resilience. They become habits that sustain you and maintain your well-being.

Affirmative routines can start early in life.

For example, every child benefits from a bedtime routine—such as a set bedtime every night, the reading of a favorite "quiet" book, the singing of a lullaby, settling into bed with a particular blanket, lights out but a night light turned on. These are signals to a child's body and spirit to start the process of personal sleep induction. This is one of the self-hypnotic functions that governs the rhythm and peaceable journey of life. Wise parents initiate rituals for bedtimes and many other things.

Laying down similar routines in your own life and in the lives of those you love help you weather the storms of change and return to "change resilience ground zero." You will maintain personal peace and focus when life slams you through its hell-for-leather and zigzag turns, bringing you back to your center-of-balance, like the professional bobsled driver who leans just so, as the bobsled careens down the track slicing back and forth across the face of the mountain.

A routine is a process. A process is an interconnected series of steps producing a desired outcome.

To establish a process, decide on the desired outcome, then list the steps that lead to the outcome. Then make it easy to take the first two or three steps. For example, if your desired outcome is to jog every morning, you might lay out your jogging clothes and shoes the night before. Wake up at the appropriate time, put on the clothes, step out the door, stretch, start walking. Soon you will be off and running. Literally.

Family traditions also serve as routines. They sustain you through change's storms. But your traditions must be started, kept, and guarded. And changed when needed. Our annual end-of-summer family whipped cream fights in the front yard had to cease when the intensity upset our youngest. We started other traditions instead. Even when no longer practiced, the mere memory of these routines evokes a feeling of peace and life-groundedness.

Baseline preparation also serves as a life and sanity-sustaining thread. For example, distance runners put in a lot of slow(er) miles to lay down a foundation of fitness before they start their speed work. So do competitive bicyclists. So do concert pianists and computer genius-geeks. Researchers estimate it takes

10,000 hours of solid practice to lay the foundation for genius. This equates to five years fulltime, ten years half-time. It takes the same to lay down a life foundation for change resilience. But once laid down, the set of habits provides solid under-footing forever.

Threads of stability can become incantations of substantial power. They are available, like magical spells, whenever you need their power. You simply need to find or invent them. Each practice evokes strength and constant creative power in the face of change and enables you to transmute the energy of change into forces and products that benefit you and those you care about.

Employ previous principles in this book to bring as many things to closure and create as many threads of stability as possible. Open items, unmade decisions, unresolved relationships create tension and siphon off energy. Attach these items to a routine and the routine will help you resolve them and keep things moving forward.

Take time to "waste" time. This may sound contradictory, but with every crop, there is a time of planting, a time of harvest, and a time of lying fallow—a time when the ground is not being worked, but instead allowed to rest. All of these times are important to the final product. All are part of a rhythm. Let your life rest from time to time.

Be aware that some routines are not positive. In fact, they are decidedly negative. For example, addictions and lazy habits negate progress. They close down relationships, limit capacity, subvert accomplishments, and can become all-encompassing life-drains. You might call these threads of instability. They are to be avoided as the dark imitations of positive routine. If you are caught in one, seek counsel. Ask a friend or a professional what you could or should do differently. Accept help. Seek inspiration. Persist in following through.

LIFE TOOLS™
Use consistently until they become your tools for life

1. Establish an exercise routine. Include stretching, aerobic, strength, and balanced movement, such as that provided by sports or yoga. Exercise a minimum of three times per week.

2. Establish an inspirational reading and meditation and decision-making routine. Employ this routine at a time of personal alertness. For some this

is first thing in the morning; for others it is a quiet time before going to bed. During this interlude, look for inspiration, think through priorities, evaluate your progress, make decisions, and set new direction. Be consistent for 21 days, or until it becomes a habit.

3. Identity five or six threads of stability (routine habits) that are currently alive in your life. What are they and why do they exist? When did they start? Do they still serve their purpose? If you are not sure, experiment with changing them.

4. Each life needs an intelligent mixture of routine and spontaneity. Sometimes routine lays the foundation or structure to jump off into spontaneity. Decide if you have the right mix in your life. If you think the mix is off, either add more routine, or add more spontaneity.

5. Ask three people you trust if they would rate your life is too bound up in routine, or not structured enough. Decide how much of their perception is valid. Write down your conclusions and take corrective action accordingly.

6. Invent a ritual as a trigger to your creativity. Try it over a period of days. Decide if it serves you. If not, invent and employ another.

7. Start a new family tradition. Or a tradition with your spouse or significant other or a family member. Or a friend (friend tradition). Notice the comfort and reassurance this brings.

8. Make a list of goals, or refer to a list you created earlier. Pick one or two important ones that require consistent persistence. Write down the two or three actions that you think will initiate the process of goal accomplishment in this area. Employ this method at least three times to assess if it invokes the process of completion.

TRAPS

Do not resist the change of changing a routine. The progression of life on this planet renders almost all routines obsolete eventually. Be prepared to let go and let them die, to make room for new habits of stability.

Your first tries might fail or fall short. Don't give up at the first attempt. Persist through discouragement. Learn and progress. Be courageous. Persist through the awkwardness of new behavior. Try twice. Or thrice.

Resistance to sudden, unexpected change is often a signal of a wonderful opportunity at hand, and that you need a new set of behaviors (stability thread).

PERPETUAL ENCOURAGEMENT

Do not procrastinate. Procrastination is the thief of happiness. Stand up now, and start!

You have power. You have a divine right to your own choices and actions. What you decide, and what you do, is valid. If new behavior does not serve you and those you love, you will know soon enough, and you can adjust.

Try new things. You can always shift if it does not work. You will learn from anything new that you attempt.

APPENDIX

Begin to invoke the power of new routine. Examples are:

- For seven days straight, tell someone why you love them
- Eat "healthy" for seven days
- Establish a monthly get-together with a friend.
- Start a club or group.
- Sign up for an exercise class. Establish a room or a space that invokes certain feelings or thought patterns.
- Hang a picture on the wall or refrigerator door.
- Read a book of daily meditations.
- Make a list of things to be done that day, every day.
- Follow the same routine each day with your to-do list.
- Clear clutter, except for what is most relevant.
- Place your furniture in a new configuration.
- Buy or borrow a new tool.
- Start a garden.
- Buy a plant and keep it alive.
- Acquire a pet and take care of it. Establish a morning time for inspiration and planning

SUMMARY

1. Threads of stability are positive routines, rituals, and processes that fill in gaps in motivation and clarity and carry you in good trim through challenging times of change.

2. Decide on routines that will serve you, and carry them through. If you do one for 21 days, it becomes a habit.

3. There are any number of practices that can become positive routines—inspirational reading and meditation, planning, a weekly phone call to a loved one or a coach.

4. You must guard against routines becoming ruts (a grave with both ends open). Identify and abandon ruts. You must likewise guard against being caught in and allowing yourself to stay a prisoner of addiction and laziness.

5. Many routines are processes. A process is a series of interconnected steps leading to a desired outcome. You can benefit by laying down a path in advance to make it easy for you to take the first two steps. Then you are off and running with the other steps.

6. Family traditions are threads of stability. Laying down a baseline of preparation is a thread, like a concert pianist or a distance runner or bicyclist at the beginning of a training regimen. So is "wasting time" at the beginning of a process or accomplishment, to figure things out and give you the mindset to continue on a chosen path.

7. Do not procrastinate laying down positive routines to push and pull you through times of turbulence.

PRINCIPLE 16:

Exert Intentionality

To exert intentionality is to create a preferred future. Insistent intentions are especially powerful and important during times of challenging change. They become pinpoints of light that coalesce into our North Star, pointing the way to peace and accomplishment. Through power-of-intentionality, we focus all of the productive, evocative, creative skill and power that we possess. Bad times become good times. Being intentional nurtures hope and causes constancy amid change. It feeds our mind and soul and spirit.

SONGLINE
Learn to navigate the wilderness of change

As I was graduating from my first college in 1971, I pondered a great deal on what to do as a vocation. I decided that I wanted to do three different things in the next ten years, though I did not prescribe each of the three career goals; I just set that diversity as a ten year goal. A large part of my intention was to prepare myself to be an effective counselor to others in their careers and lives. Then I "filed" the paper and forgot about it. Ten years later I was going through some old papers and ran across the intentionality that I had committed to paper.

I had exactly accomplished my intention: (1) I had engaged in a "real" job as a sales rep with Procter & Gamble, (2) I had been a faculty member at a respected university and (3) I was now in a high impact position with a Fortune 50 company.

From all of these experiences, I had gained knowledge and perspective to allow me to be a superb counselor to others. Some of these had seemed accidental at the time; all had been part of my personal path of intentionality. All had been accomplished through change, sometimes heart- wrenching change, often straight into the teeth of fear. But as it had turned out, all had been a part of a larger intentionality.

The power of the human mind to exert constant and powerful intentionality is demonstrated by the fixation of thought that often precedes a new purchase, such as an automobile. Once our mind is fastened on a certain make and model, suddenly everywhere we turn that model is humming along beside us and in front of us on the roadway. We also see it on television, in movies, in magazines, on the web. We notice it time and time again, and wonder at the phenomenon. Reality has not changed; our intentionality has changed, and we see with new eyes what was there all along. This awareness is a harbinger of successful completion of the intention.

Intentionality is the primary source of power. It is the prime source of being and action. Intentionality focuses on things that can be, thinking of them as if they will be. Intentionality brings forth reality. It transforms inner reality into outer reality.

Intentionality creates pathways of action. We see things to be done that we did not see before. We know to ask for help in ways that we did not know before.

Avenues are opened to us that were not open before. The way is made sure.

My daughter once set her intention to go to a foreign land and provide multi-years of service to the people there. She announced this to everyone, making it a public declaration, and proceeded to prepare. She determined to save money to pay her own way. One way she did that was to waitress at Outback restaurant. She was an attractive, attentive, and personable waitress, and earned good tips.

The Wisdom of K. Hieronymus

Maintaining a continuity of openness, meekness and lowliness in our inner being allows the continual intelligent exercise of intentionality and enjoyment of its fruits. Placing the personal gift of a broken heart and a contrite spirit on the altar of life lays the foundation for the perfect exercise of intentionality.

One tip was especially good. One evening an older gentleman gave her cash in the amount of $50 more than the amount of the meal. When she discovered the overage, she returned it to him, explaining his error. He said, "It was not a mistake. You need that money." She resisted, and he reiterated, "No, you need that money. Take it." She did, and brought her intended mission that much closer. She eventually fulfilled that mission, very successfully.

Effective intentions must be real and personal. We do it for ourselves, though often to the benefit of others. They come from our heart and soul. They point the way to the future. They create a tingling excitement. But they are often preceded, or accompanied, by fear.

Fear means one of two things. Either the thing we are intending is inherently dangerous or stupid, ergo, something we should refrain from doing, and we should stop immediately, or... the thing we are intending is so large, so on-track and so audacious that it scares us. We are not sure we are a big enough person. We are tempted to retreat to the comfort of playing small. Absent true danger, the right answer is to persist, courageously, in the face of fear. We must recognize that courage is not the absence of fear, but the absence of retreat in the face of fear.

Rightly-focused intentionality feeds our positive emotions. As we come to understand the true nature of intentionality, we naturally begin to replace all feelings of doubt, fear, anger, jealousy, and pride with loving, affirmative emotions. We come to possess full confidence and trust in the rightness of our purpose.

Usually it is sufficient to start the first step. One step creates energy for the next, like climbing a mountain. When we reach what we thought was the summit, we have a point of view. We see the real summit ahead of us, one that we could not see before. The beauty of the new vista pulls us forward, like a magnet, to the promise of the higher ground. And then, before our feet, through the rocks, we see a path upward that we could not see before.

Positive intentionality is the counterpoint to unexpected and unwelcome change, the jutting prow of the elegant ship that cuts through the tumultuous cacophony of the waves of change. That said, at times we must endure the waves for some time before the time is right to exert our intentions. Sometimes it takes more courage and as much wisdom to wait as to act.

APPLICATION
Employ this principle to benefit you and those you love

Intentionality, by definition, can be intentionally mobilized. It begins with desires and goals; it proceeds according to fulfillment structures.

The power of intentionality is first fueled by simple desire. In some cases, to start, it is enough to simply desire that something be. The desire may be tiny at first. But let the desire work in you: attend to it, cultivate it, talk about it, focus on it, make a visual collage, build a model, create or obtain a brochure, look forward to it, think about it, and talk about it as if it were already true.

For example, if you desire a new car, feel your hands wrapped around the steering wheel. If you desire a relationship, imagine the eye contact, the clasped hands, the conversations and feelings you will have. If you desire a chance to render greater service, see yourself in your mind's eye proffering that service.

Make the declaration regarding the future state, then proceed as if it were true. Set the table for the meal you intend to have, lay down enough fine china for the number of guests you intend to attend. Put out the best silverware.

Pay attention to your wants and needs. Wants and needs are the servants of intentionality. They are the promise of what may come in your life. You need certain things for survival; you need certain things for well-being, change, resilience, and growth. Some wants are really needs; some are not. Learn to ask and work for what you want. Thus you will discover what is really a need. Dare to hope for the fulfillment of your wants and needs.

Intentionality does not stand alone. It is always bound together with hope. As you begin to exert intentionality, you humbly yet resolutely fasten your mind with great tenacity onto something strongly hoped for, with such mental intensity and "pre-knowledge" that it is as if the reality of that thing were already in existence.

The terminally ill understand this. Once they come to grips with the crushing challenge of the massive change/knowledge of a set amount of time left in this life, they start to focus on what really matters. A short time frame concentrates the mind wonderfully. Act as if time is running out. Because it always is.

Getting started is important. Planning, though important, and a way to avoid missteps and wasted time, should not be overdone to the exclusion of just taking the first step.

At the first step, you gain capacity and see applications that you could not see before and that can only be seen from a new vantage point.

Sometimes, to get started, you must first acknowledge your weakness in the area of your desire; then get moving.

Your capacity will grow with each step. Continuing to step forward with intentional focus and action carries you through the whitewater of your change challenges.

As you push forward in intentionality, you will often see rocks in the road. When you have a setback or get stuck, like the turtle stuck in the wire fence described in an earlier module, reframe the event. When you lack knowledge, pick up a book or talk to a teacher. When you are confused, write down your top three priorities. When you don't know how to proceed, answer the first five project organization questions. When the change seems unbearable, categorize it according to the four types, from an earlier principle, and take the approach warranted.

Vision is a component of intentionality. When you take the time to look, you will see things that you did not have time to see before. The goal is clearer, like the suddenly sunlit meadow of possibility spread out before you as the light of hope bursts through a hole in the departing storm clouds.

You often do just enough to get by. And sometimes just to do that is an enormous and laudable effort. But really living life in all of its possibility means looking at a much bigger picture, seeing with the perspective of how you can thrive beyond the set of circumstances that you see. This self-chosen "illusion" is an illusion that creates reality. When you find yourself thinking "survival," think bigger. Stand on the rock of intention. Doing so gives you a larger perspective.

To exert intentionality means to live way beyond survival—not just thinking "How do I keep from getting fired, how do I survive this meeting, how do I survive these teenagers or how do I make it through this change?". You must look beyond survival to a vision of the future, to not just surviving but thriving in some future state. The vision gives you everything you need to be able to say, "Here is the path. Here is the summit. And here is my energy."

Be prepared that not all intentionality brings forth change that is desirable or comfortable. But sometimes the change is necessary. Sometimes your life must be broken up, the house of your being must be demolished in a spot or two in the process of your soul's remodeling.

Doubts and fears are the great enemies of intentionality. Face them, and examine their validity.

Gratitude for the fruits of intentionality insures their continuance. When you savor what you already have, your mind automatically looks forward to more. Counting blessings creates more blessings.

Gratitude is a prime energy source for further positive creation. Energy for more good will come your way.

You also will benefit by noticing and appreciating the good intentions of others; indeed, you usually benefit by always assuming positive intent in others' actions. Their intention becomes part of your larger, positive intention.

One last note: unhealthy obsession is the dark side of intentionality. Be certain that you are not hanging on to a desire way beyond the point of utility

LIFE TOOLS™
Use consistently until they become your tools for life

1. Take stock of the elements of your life. Make a list of the areas where you are just "surviving," just getting by. Your list of stewardships from the earlier "Embrace Stewardship" principle might be a good starting point. Using a writing element different from your norm, whether a pen, pencil, marker, or crayon, draw a picture of what things would look like if you were in "breakthrough mode," not just getting by. Or you can cut pictures out of magazines that represent the flip side of survival, thriving. Post this picture where you can see it. Be open to new thoughts and make a determined effort to try something different. As you experience doubts and fears, keep moving.

2. Make a four-column table. In the first column, list all of your doubts and fears. Be comprehensive. Try for more than 10. In the second column, next to each entry, write what you would be saying to yourself if you did not have that doubt or fear. In the third column, write the realistic description of why that fear or doubt has some validity—what does it point to that you might wisely take into account. In the fourth column, write what you would be doing if you did not have that doubt or fear. Then, courageously do three of the things in the fourth column. You may do more if you wish. Write down what you learn from this experience.

3. Write down experiences and events you intend to do (fewer than five) in the next 10 years. Then file away the paper. You know the rest of that story.

4. Take notes on a person you admire for their confidence and capacity to accomplish. "Interview" them: ask them about a time when they had to overcome doubt or fear. Ask them how they came to acquire these attributes.

5. What is not going well in your life? What do you want instead? List three things. For a few days, think a lot about what you want in these three areas. Tell a friend.

6. Ask someone who cares about you what they desire for your life. Listen carefully. Write it down. Read it often.

7. Create a bulletin board with pictures or statements about your desires, hopes and goals for the future. Schedule a time on your calendar, however short, to look at the bulletin board and think about these things.

TRAPS

Do not think you cannot take time to intend. Society tells us that we must be busy to be of worth. This is not true. Pause, introspect, discover, then have the temerity to announce your intentions, to revel in the (imagined) fruit of your intentions, to enlist others in the cause, if only as enthusiastic observers. You will be amazed at the results.

Your first tries will sometimes fail or fall short. Don't give up. Persist through awkwardness. Learn and progress. Be courageous. Try twice. Or thrice.

Good intentions must be fed and focused on (sometimes obsessed upon). Most importantly, they must be acted on. Then we must write them on our calendar. Otherwise they remain in the same dead category as pious hopes and fervent wishes.

PERPETUAL ENCOURAGEMENT

Do not procrastinate. Procrastination is the thief of happiness. Stand up now, and take the first step!

Do something. You cannot correct a nothing.

Intentionality is the great and original source of power, the principle from which all action and result flow and attain being. And the power for intentionality is entirely in your possession.

Intentionality sets things in motion. Intentions come first, not something else. As you exert intentionality, you stride forward into the path of your life. The sequence is: "I can, I must, I will, I am (doing)."

APPENDIX

Happiness consists of having something to do, something to look forward to, and someone to love. The "look forward to" part is the realm of intentionality.

"Concerning all acts of initiative and creation, there is one elementary truth— that the moment one definitely commits oneself, then Providence moves too."
- **W. H. Murray**, The Story of Everest

I believe that I am always Divinely guided.

I believe that I will always take the right road.

I believe that God will always make a way where there is no way.

(Commander William Robert Anderson kept this saying in his hip pocket in process of taking the submarine Nautilus under the Antarctic)

C. S. Lewis spoke of remodeling. Google it.

SUMMARY

1. Through power-of-intentionality, we focus and encapsulate all of the productive, evocative, creative skill, and power that we possess, turning bad times into good times.

2. Insistent intentions are especially powerful and important during times of challenging change. Being intentional causes constancy amid change.

3. The power of intentionality begins with a strong belief or desire that something be true, which results in focused, hopeful, energetic thought, accompanied by vigorous and diligent action, as if one had strong evidence. We must keep our minds firmly and positively focused on the object of our desire, and speak of it with positive expectation.

4. Intentions must be sincere to be effective, not just a good idea we heard somewhere or that someone wants us to do. We do it for ourselves, though often to the benefit of others.

5. Real intentionality creates a tingling excitement. But it is often preceded, or accompanied, by fear.

6. Fear is a sign of one of two things. Either the thing we are intending is inherently dangerous or stupid, ergo, something we should stop immediately, or the thing we are intending is so large, so on-track and so audacious that it scares us. We are not sure we are a big enough person. Absent true danger, the right answer is—to jump, to courageously push forward in the face of fear. We must recognize that courage is not the absence of fear, but the absence of inaction in the face of fear.

7. Our continual and intentional focus and action will carry us through the whitewater of change challenges.

8. Consistent actions, however small, combine to create unstoppable momentum. As we act persistently on our intentionality, every event and interaction serves to propel us farther down the road to accomplish our desire.

IN THE END:

Establish Sustainability

CONGRATULATIONS!! YOU ARE A FINISHER!

It has been quite a process. And you have been quite a student.

You have persisted for many weeks and are close to finishing the program on Personal Change Resilience. You have courageously tackled the task of learning (or learning more deeply) sixteen principles that enable you to proactively transmute the energy of change to your personal good and to the welfare of those you love.

There were times when you struggled to grasp and apply the principles.

There were times when it took courage to move ahead and try new things.

There were times when your life was full of challenges and distractions that ate up, it seemed, all of your spare time. Still you persisted.

There were times that you did not fully complete the principle. Or you felt that something, in some way, was incomplete. Yet you still persisted and progressed, at times in ways that are not yet expressed fully in your life.

There were times when you felt you were behind, that you weren't doing enough or that what you did wasn't good enough. NOT TRUE. You have accomplished a tremendous amount. And all along, you have been developing your change resilience muscle. This will serve you well in the future.

WHAT YOU HAVE LEARNED

- You have learned to accept change—all change—as a positive life force.

- You have learned how to stir yourself to try new things.

- You have learned that all change creates energy that can be molded to positive personal and familial and social ends. You have learned to discern the four types of change: Welcome-Expected, Welcome-Unexpected, Unwelcome-Expected, Unwelcome-Unexpected. You have learned different strategies for coping with and extracting/expressing the energy from each type of change.

- You have pushed through your fears and doubts. You have stepped outside your comfort zone time and again.

- You have learned to embrace your personal stewardships and to take on positive stress as your partner in productive change.

- You have learned to magnify your self-esteem to your good and the good of others.

- You have learned how to invent projects, create fulfillment structures, and drive to closure.

Also, you have:

- Embraced the law of the harvest.

- Identified your empowering life assumptions and brought them to tighter focus in your life.

- Deepened some relationships, ended others. All to the good.

- Exerted intentionality.

- Committed to learn constantly, even as you have pursued development of personal talent.

- Learned or relearned the power of cultivating humor, and of reframing bad/good.

- Created threads of stability to carry you through times of challenging change.

- Learned the power of a personal reminder system as a means of keeping you on track and continually progressing, and gained skill in keeping yourself focused and productive.

In sum, and most important, you have developed your Personal Change Resilience. In powerful and subtle ways, you have increased your personal capacity to transmute the energy of change to the benefit of yourself and those you love.

Some of this newly-acquired strength will not become evident until a new change challenge plops itself at your doorstep (or pounces on your head or sneaks under your pillow). Or, using the outlook and tools you have acquired and polished, you will be the origin and architect of change.

You have new tools and a new commitment to not become overwhelmed at volume, size, or sheer noise of the changes that will both hammer and bless you all the remaining days of your life. Storms of change will come. When you practice the principles, you become the eye (the "I") of the storm. Others will seek to share in your serenity and power. You now have tools at your disposal that others will want to borrow.

You have one thing yet to learn. You are about to learn how to sustain the progress you have made. You are about to learn the three steps to nurturing sustainability.

Sustaining positive change is a lifelong task, an enjoyable though not always easy path to constant improvement, fresh perspective, and joy.

Take the following three steps to create sustainability.

STEP 1: TACKLE A REAL, LIVE CHANGE CHALLENGE

Let's get started in turning what could be bad times, into good times. Thinking about the change challenges in your life, or the change challenges coming down the pike, make a list. List the things in your life that confound you, or that confront you with a change that is hard to handle. One challenge might come from a person close to you, another might be something outward and physical that needs attention; another might be a personal challenge: perhaps a large jump needed in capacity, patience, or self-discipline.

For example, perhaps there is something that needs to be done before winter sets in, a building or an item to be winterized. Something with a deadline. Something difficult that will take extra effort. Perhaps something that will take expertise and strength beyond what you currently possess.

For me, because of a change in the condition of my freestanding garage, I could choose as my change challenge a garage door that needs new trim and caulk before cold, moisture, and ice grab hold in earnest.

I am getting ahead of myself, but I could apply two change principles—first, to treat this as a project and apply the principles accordingly; second, to kindle a relationship with someone with more expertise, so the repair is done well. I also will likely need to borrow tools.

Another example—because of a change in my family situation, I need to lay in some firewood for the winter. I know of a free source, compliments of a local tree-trimming company. But there are arrangements to be made, transport and splitting to be lined out.

These would be on my list. Now, make your own list, somewhere between three and five items. The holiday season often brings relationship issues to the forefront. One of the items on your list might jump out as the prime target for your current efforts. If not, then mark the top three in terms of the consternation they cause you or the strength of your desire to do something about them. Then pick one. This is your "practice problem."

Keeping your problem in mind, go back through the change principles and pick one or more that apply to this problem. When you have "discovered" the principles, extract points for action and write down the first three steps. Then get started. This will unleash the energy of action. Momentum will take hold.

STEP 2: SUSTAIN POSITIVE CHANGE

Take these actions to sustain the changes you have made and to lay the foundation for future progress:

Read back through the reports you have written. Write a short paragraph or a set of five or ten bullet points that describe what you have learned during this year-long experience.

Or, if it works better for you, print a fresh copy of all the modules and highlight the passages that speak most meaningfully to you.

In any case, do three things next: make a one-page summary of the learning points and post them where you will see them frequently. If you prepared it earlier, print out a list of your empowering life assumptions (in principle 2) and put them with your learning points, where you will see them often. Also, print the page in listing the four types of change and the recommended responses to each (also in principle 2).

STEP 3: PUT REMINDERS ON YOUR CALENDAR

- Obtain a calendar covering at least the next six months.
- Beyond the change challenges you have already listed, list the change(s) that will likely occur in your life in the next six months. List the type of change.
- List at least one life tool that makes sense to be applied to each of the changes.

ADDENDUM

IN THE FUTURE, APPLY THE FOLLOWING EIGHT CHANGE STABILIZATION STEPS WHEN A CHANGE "HITS" YOU (OR WHEN YOU PURPOSELY HIT CHANGE):

1. What is the change? Describe it in a word or phrase.

2. Take stock—As best you can tell, what is the immediate, true situation? When you look at each facet of the change and the impact, what is truly at risk? Will you die (you might)—or is it not really life-and-death this

time? What is lost, and can you handle it? What type is this change (1-4)? What change resilience strategies are indicated? What might be the positives of this change?

3. Look at your list of empowering life assumptions. Which will come into play during this event? Which will be required to strengthen and sustain you? Print off your list in a large font. Highlight the five or six that will be especially valuable in this challenge. Place this list in a prominent place to remind you of the things you already know and the power these assumptions bring into your minute-to-minute life.

4. Stabilize and triage—Are there any stopgap measures that you should put in place right now? Are there people to be asked for help or support? What are the priorities?

5. Take the long view—In five years, how will you or might you view this change? Ask the same question for ten years. For 20 years. Identify your tools—What change principle(s) will be best applied to this situation?

6. Take action—One prime action might be to ask for help. Another might be to wait. Or the best option might be to set a path (sometimes deciding the first two steps suffices) and to act with vigor and spear-point focus.

7. Now take stock again—Where are you now? What is next?

8. (Alternative to Steps 1-3 above)—First print out the modules and place them in a binder. Or you may use an electronic copy for this exercise.

Then pick your Personal "Best of the Best":

- Go back through the Life Tools you have applied to pick the "best of the best" for you and your current life situation.
  - ✓ Pick five things that stand out for you and you want to apply.
  - ✓ Write them down on a sheet of paper.
  - ✓ Write down what you will do to apply each one.

- Put this sheet in a secure place where you can refer to it. Write down a date during each quarter of the coming year when you will take it out and "re-up".

What "re-upping" looks like: for each date written on your calendar, set a specific time of day for a one-hour meeting with yourself to revisit the sheet you just created. Make the last appointment for sometime before American Thanksgiving. When the time for your appointment arrives, haul out the sheet you prepared. Look it over and do whatever is suggested to your mind.

You may desire to pull out the sheet and look at it more often: new circumstances of change will call for new strength, which you have already acquired through your diligent work with these principles. Reading the sheet reminds you of the strength you already possess, and you will notice ideas to apply.

Sustainability is the most important part of change resilience. Change will not cease. You can choose to hunker down and hide, in which case the waves of change will still find you, pound down the walls of your bunker and tumble you like a batch of clothes in the wash. Or you can choose to face change proactively and gain strength, new knowledge, and power to bless others.

Change is the universe's most valuable gift to your future. Treasure it. Use its energy wisely.

EPILOGUE

Almost exactly four years ago today, Lin departed for her new sphere of action.

Things now are much different. I have spent much time in the Wilderness of Change. I have tested and retested my Personal Change Resilience. The wilderness topography itself has changed:

- I am in a new relationship.

- I tried my hand at a number of things; none were my calling.

- I live in a new house, in a new town.

- I am in a new career—as a professor of business (my calling) at the university in that town (Warrensburg, Missouri). The University of Central Missouri. I chose Red. The Mules. I teach leadership and strategy in the B-school.

I wish I could say that I have impeccably performed as stated in the last paragraphs of this book's prologue, i.e., that I would have my life be an unbroken, grand parade. Not true. The weather after Lin's death was as changeable as weather always is, and I did not always shelter myself felicitously: days of brilliant sunshine, days of soft breezes and days of calm alternated with day after unending day of dreary gray clouds, great storms with piercing lightning, with thunder and pounding rain, and somber days of misty rain, times when the weather could not make up its mind what to do, strong headwinds, quartering side winds, punchy tailwinds.

In short, life in the wilderness continued to assert itself, and gave rise to all manner of mood.

The change from then to now stands in stark contrast. Then, holidays were torture. Mornings often gray and dead. New relationships, tho in the main positive and numerous, were nerve-wracking and tenuous. Now, most days, I wake up with a smile on my face. And fall asleep the same.

One thread of stability now over-arches all:

Before Lin left, she "commanded" me to remarry. Without telling me, she put my daughter, Kadra, in charge of watching over me. She told me what kind of woman I would marry. She laid out the formula... I complied as best I could.

I met, wooed and wed (or was it the other way around?) a woman of delight and generosity... introduced by my daughter, Kadra (who else?); a woman willing to move from Portland, Oregon to the Midwest.

Jo Anne is delightful, supportive, generous, well traveled, well read, a lover of music and beautiful things, and ferocious in defending those things she loves. I am lucky to be counted among those things. She brings an energy into our life together that is distinctive, filled with intelligence and intensely encouraging.

We look forward to an eternal future together. We are making our home in the country in the near-center of Missouri, in what I have come to call Jurassic Forest (big and many bugs). We have a lovely house, lovely cats and dogs, lovely and lively fish in our pond surrounded by Rocky Mountain granite. I am blessed.

We knew within weeks of our introduction, via email and phone, by my daughter Kadra in Portland, Oregon, that we had to meet each other. The story of that swift courtship is a different story, to be told later, at length and elsewhere. Last night, as we were re-watching "My Big Fat Greek Wedding", as this book is about to go to press, we commented on how perfect our courtship and marriage were, how well suited to our personalities, and how well expressed and received.

Two poems I have written express the path through the wilderness, the contrast from then to now the last four years. One poem is of enduring pain; one of energy and hope. I will end this epilogue with these poems:

The Discipline of Pain

"Deep clouds of pain
Make me want to
Slip away
From the torture
Of the suture
To reality"

"What awful prophecy
Have I wrapped around me
What terrible necessity
Haunts my destiny"

"A carven stake
Pierces my heart
Pins me to holy earth
Perhaps that I do not
Flee
Utmost possibility"

"The leaden days
The pallid nights
Suspended
From threads of pain
In earthen jar
Swinging"

"As the softly sighing
Beast of pain
Trudges
Endless
In my brain"

I Ran

I ran

Far past the sun

I ran til my limbs and loins

Were vague remembrances

Far past that point did I run

Far past and back again around past the point of no return

I ran the clouds away

Til the sky was cleared of all remorse and nonsense

I ran

I ran past the gilt shadows of the torrid evening
I ran past the sorrows embedded in the concrete
I ran past the wet winds lancing the swollen night
I ran past the corner of the trembling saints
I ran past the music of the terrible angel voices
I ran past all poetry

I ran laughing breakneck into the purple dawn

Lorin Walker

Jurassic Forest, Warrensburg Missouri

May 12, 2015

ABOUT THE AUTHOR

Lorin Walker, PhD, has been counseling and coaching individuals and corporate leaders and teams for three decades. He has worked fulltime for several Fortune 100 companies: Procter & Gamble, ARCO Oil and Gas, and Ernst & Young. He has consulted to over 70 different corporations and public entities across the world, including LinkedIn, Shell Canada, Bechtel, Southland Corporation, Banc One, KPMG, Chevron, Canon Imaging Systems, Worley Parsons, Dow Chemical, the Washington DC office of the Small Business Administration and the Environmental Protection Agency . He has led and trained hundreds of teams and coached and counseled thousands of individuals to higher performance.

A constant learner, Dr. Walker has consistently developed and improved a change methodology for precise, quick and lasting results. Together with his spouse and seven children, his activity in family, business and community endeavors keeps him highly attuned to the special challenges of our times.

Lorin is also exceptionally well prepared academically to lead a program on change resilience and growth. He received his undergraduate degree from Columbia University in New York City. He earned an MA in Organizational Behavior, with honors, at the Marriott School of Management at Brigham Young University, and a PhD in Counseling Psychology, also at Brigham Young, where he was a faculty member.

His dissertation research examined "The Relationship Between Self-esteem and Productive Change in Work Groups.

Recent articles, white papers and other publications include:

"Making Good Teams Great (with apologies to American baseball)", "Love of Design", "Self-esteem as Leadership Imperative", "Coach Me!", "Managing Change Management", "Line-Of-Sight Leadership", "Speed-to-Competence".

He enjoys bicycling, backpacking, basketball and photography. He has co-written several songs, and since July of 2007 has published a Leadership and Life Balance Blog: http://walkerswalkabout.wordpress.com .

He is currently a faculty member in the business school at the University of Central Missouri, where he teaches Leadership and Strategy.

INDEX

49220295R00112

Made in the USA
Charleston, SC
18 November 2015